LOVED BACK
to LIFE

LOVED BACK *to* LIFE

HOW I FOUND the COURAGE to LIVE FREE

SHEILA WALSH

NELSON
BOOKS

An Imprint of Thomas Nelson

Published in Nashville, Tennessee, by Nelson Books, an imprint of Thomas Nelson. Nelson Books and Thomas Nelson are registered trademarks of HarperCollins Christian Publishing, Inc.

Loved Back to Life is a revision of *Honestly*, previously published by Zondervan Publishing House (ISBNs: 9780718021870 [book]; 9780718021894 [eBook]).

Published in association with the literary agencies of Wolgemuth & Associates, Inc., and The Fedd Agency, Inc.

Thomas Nelson titles may be purchased in bulk for educational, business, fund-raising, or sales promotional use. For information, please e-mail SpecialMarkets@ ThomasNelson.com.

Unless otherwise noted, Scripture quotations are taken from the Holy Bible: New International Version®. NIV®. Copyright © 1973, 1978, 1984, 2011 by Biblica, Inc.™. Used by permission of Zondervan. All rights reserved worldwide.

Scripture quotations marked NLT are from *Holy Bible*, New Living Translation. © 1996, 2004, 2007 by Tyndale House Foundation. Used by permission of Tyndale House Publishers, Inc., Carol Stream, Illinois 60188. All rights reserved.

Scripture quotations marked ESV are from the ENGLISH STANDARD VERSION. © 2001 by Crossway Bibles, a division of Good News Publishers.

Any Internet addresses (websites, blogs, etc.) in this book are offered as a resource. They are not intended in any way to be or imply an endorsement by Thomas Nelson, nor does Thomas Nelson vouch for the content of these sites and numbers for the life of this book.

Library of Congress Control Number: 2014954524

ISBN: 978-0-7180-2187-0

Printed in the United States of America

15 16 17 18 19 RRD 6 5 4 3 2 1

This book is dedicated in memory of my darling friend, Cindy Wilt Colville. You spent your life championing others and are now in the presence of our great Champion, Jesus Christ. All who knew you well miss you deeply but all who love Christ can say with confidence, we will see you soon!

Contents

Part 3: The Road Home

Introduction

Twenty years is a long time, and yet as I think back to the night when I was admitted to the locked ward of a psychiatric hospital, it's as vivid to me now as if it were yesterday.

In the weeks and months that followed, I kept a journal. Some pages detailed my drowning days, others when there seemed to be a glimmer of daylight on the horizon. I never intended to share that scribbled journey, as it was deeply personal. I believed, too, that I was the only passenger. I didn't know of any other Christian leader who battled dark, abysmal days weighted down by severe clinical depression. But a wonderful counselor, Dr. Frank Gripka, continued to tell me I was not the only one. He said someone had to stand up and tell the truth out loud, so I thought, *Why not me?* I had nothing left to lose.

Many of those whom I thought were friends had walked

away. Mental illness had the curb appeal of the AIDS epidemic in the days before we understood that you couldn't catch it just by hugging someone who was infected. For a Christian who wrestled a disease of the mind, it was assumed that something in your behavior or a pervasive lack of faith had brought it on. We tend to walk away from what we don't understand.

So I wrote the book *Honestly*, praying that it would help even one other person who felt terminally hopeless. In 1997, I tentatively began to speak about this taboo subject from the stage, and every time I spoke the truth out loud, I would find my tribe hiding in the crowd, longing to tell their stories to one other person who understood. A lot of things have changed in the years that followed. There have been many others who have begun to speak out and demystify this illness, but the stigma remains, especially in the church. I still receive letters and texts from those who have made *Honestly* a textbook of hope, but there are always questions.

"Do you still take medication?"

"How does this affect your family?"

"Are you healed now?"

So, here we are, continuing on the journey of how God took me from a place of wanting to die to the way He continues day by day to love me back to life.

I found it hard rereading the original book. It sent me into a bit of a tailspin to remember the worst days. It made me angry, too, meeting the "me" in those pages. I was angry because I apologized for being sick. I was angry because I believed some of the garbage I was told about those who struggle with mental illness. But as I sat down to write this book, an update and continuation of my journey, the anger faded. I took a deep breath and reminded myself that I did the best I could in the darkest days of my life; that was true for many of those around me as well.

Let me take you back to where the descent began. It was dark and it was deep, but the truth that I thought would kill me actually saved my life. That's my prayer for you.

Part 1

The Volcano

On the edge of a volcano
I have lived for many years.
Now it seems the distant rumble's
getting louder in my ears.
I have tried to walk away
from broken pieces of the past,
but their edges tear my feet
like broken glass.
I have tried to push disturbing thoughts
beyond the reach of man.
I have tried to burn my bridges
but I've only burned my hand,
pushing things under the carpet
hoping that they'll go away,
but I know I'll
lose my balance
any day.

Chapter 1

The Distant Rumble

The weight of this sad time we must obey.
Speak what we feel, not what we ought to say.

—WILLIAM SHAKESPEARE, *KING LEAR*

I t was a glorious summer morning in 1992. The sun was rising over the water, and the bees were beginning to hum. I went out into the yard to fill the bird feeder and stood for a moment in the stillness.

I saw my neighbor sail off in his little crabbing boat, and I waved good morning. I wondered about his life. He was always alone, and every day he set out onto the water, the first to ripple the quiet. A solitary life. My little white dog barked at a visiting duck, but the duck seemed unimpressed.

I drank in the sounds of the lapping water as it broke on the boat dock. I imagined for a moment that I was ten years old again, home in Scotland, standing by the ocean, my place of peace.

I turned my back on the water to prepare for the day ahead.

I felt heavy inside, as if every bone in my body had turned to lead while I slept. After I showered, I took my coffee outside, and in the morning warmth I prayed a now familiar prayer: "God, please help me get through one more day."

It was a lovely drive from my house to the television studios where I worked. I left early enough each morning to avoid the rush of traffic. As I drove through the main gates of the Christian Broadcasting Network (CBN), I thought again how strange it was to find myself in Virginia Beach, as cohost of *The 700 Club*.

I had moved to Los Angeles from England in 1986. I had been a contemporary Christian artist since my early twenties traveling around the world, but my new record company was based in LA, and most of my current touring was in the United States, so it made sense to make this my home. I had fallen in love with this country instantly. I loved the hope that seemed to be part of the fabric of the people.

In 1988, one of the guest coordinators at CBN saw me being interviewed on a morning show, a Canadian program called *100 Huntley Street*, which broadcast extensively to certain markets across America. She taped the interview and showed it to Dr. Pat Robertson, the president of CBN, who was looking for someone to fill the position of cohost for their flagship show, *The 700 Club*. The network flew me in to meet with Pat and to audition for the position. I came armed with three "Christian" dresses from Laura Ashley. If you've ever been in one of her stores you know what I mean—flowers, flowers, and more flowers!

I had worked for three years with the British Broadcasting Corporation (BBC) in London, but this was very different. I was used to taping shows in advance, so that if anything went wrong, there was time to correct it. This was a live show, and because it was live, it was hard to rehearse. The afternoon I arrived, the producer enlisted the help of a secretary for me to "practice on." But I asked such goofy questions we spent more time laughing than rehearsing.

The next morning was the real thing. I was taken to makeup at 7:00 a.m., and by the time I left, my face felt as if it had been freshly plastered. I was definitely made-up! My hair no longer had an opinion; it was set in stone and larger than life.

Pat arrived a few minutes before the show started and prayed with six of us in his dressing room. Then we were on. I was petrified. Within minutes it became apparent to me that I was supposed to be fairly fluent in world events. But when Pat asked me about my perspective on the current situation on the West Bank in Israel, my mind went blank and I lamely replied, "I'm with the Bank of America!"

Despite the fact that I was obviously not the Scottish Barbara Walters, I was hired that day. A month later I moved from the West Coast to Virginia Beach.

I loved my job and the stimulation of discussing pressing issues with prominent church leaders and theologians. I subscribed to *The Economist* and brushed up on American history and world events. As a student at London Bible College, I had been constantly challenged to open my mind to the input of other believers whose experience of God was a little different from mine. I like to live with mystery. And every day I interviewed some of my spiritual heroes such as Billy Graham, Charles Colson, Elizabeth Elliot, and countless others.

On the surface I had it made, and everything looked fine—but I was not fine. I had not been fine for a long time. Even surrounded by others, I felt isolated. Trapped by a suffocating anxiety. Restless, though I couldn't say why. Numbed by a frantic pace. I felt as if I was slowly losing my mind.

Life, like a volcano, seems to offer early warning signals. Long before a volcano blows, there are signs that the level of activity under the surface has increased. Distant noises and rumbles become more pronounced, and that was certainly true for the sickening stirrings in my own soul.

Questions Unanswered

There were many areas of my life that did not always make sense to me. I loved my job. I loved being able to talk about the love of God to the millions who watched every day. And I received hundreds of letters from viewers telling me how the show impacted their lives. I knew this was true, but sometimes I felt like a second-hand car salesman; I had a sickening sense that what I just sold people may not get them all the way home.

Many of our viewers were very sick and longed to be healed. I believed, and still believe, without a shadow of a doubt, that God is able to do anything. He only has to speak a word and disease is gone. But, at least for the moment, in America those miraculous healings are the exception rather than the rule. Day after day many people wait, wondering if this will be "their day." If it's not, they wonder what is wrong with them. Some people claim that if you have not been healed, it is your fault; you have unconfessed sin, or you are harboring resentment toward someone.

I realize that the Bible is very clear on our responsibility to confess our sins to one another and to pray for one another so that we may be healed. But what do we say to the many people who love God passionately, who have done all that they know to do, and still are not healed? I'm afraid we either doubt their efficacy in confession, or we simply walk away and say nothing. How barbaric we can be in our perception of faith, how brutal in our pursuit of the miraculous.

It was a privilege to be part of a ministry that reached out across the world and affected the lives of so many, but I used to wonder about the viewers who watched from a wheelchair or a hospital bed. Was I helping them in their journey or making them feel more alone? I once received a letter from a young girl who was losing her battle with cancer. She watched the show every day. Sometimes it helped her, she said, and other times she wanted to take her shoe off and throw it through the screen. "You show me people every day who have been healed, and I thank God with you, but you never talk about people like me, who love God but who are dying and are trying in the midst of it all to live and die in a way that would honor Him. We are part of the family too." I was torn by her cry for dignity and acknowledgment.

Downward Spiral

I realized then that there are no quick, easy answers for any of us—even for myself. Rumblings preceded the volcanic explosion in my life. But for now I will simply say that my life blew apart when the volcano erupted in 1992, and what I had feared the most happened.

At that time I kept an utterly impossible schedule. Most weeks I was at the studio from Monday through Friday, 7:00 a.m. till 6:00 p.m. After the show was over on Friday, I would tear out of the studio to catch a flight to wherever my concert was that evening. I would usually have a Friday concert in one city and a Saturday concert in another. I would often get back to Virginia Beach at 11:00 p.m. on Sunday night, and Monday would begin the whole process all over again.

As I look back now, I ask myself why I never stopped to breathe, why I pushed myself so punishingly hard. A large part of it was simply that during those moments when I would stand onstage and talk about the love of God, I felt alive, hopeful; I knew that with God anything was possible. But when the lights went down and the people went home, I felt powerless to grasp hold of those truths for my own life. I could see dimly where I was, and I knew where I wanted to be, but I had no map to get there.

At times I tried to arrest the manic pace of my life, but it's hard to stop a train that is moving so fast. It's easier to just hold on tightly.

By the spring of that eventful year, I knew my grip was weakening. I felt numb and old and distanced from people. I would wake up in a hotel room on a weekend when I was traveling and wonder where I was. Sometimes I would be physically sick before I could pull myself together enough to get ready for a concert.

When I wasn't working, I resorted to an old, familiar habit—walking the beach. On a sunny summer day, I'd be surrounded by laughing children, dogs chasing Frisbees, and radios blaring the latest songs. But I was cold inside, as if the winter wind had never left and was seeping into my bones. My thoughts were slow and labored. I wasn't eating much at all. I would come home from work and lie in a dark room, but I could not sleep.

Sometimes, instead of tossing and turning or staring blankly at the ceiling, I would walk for miles along the beach at five or six o'clock in the morning. But though I was surrounded with beauty, with glorious sunrises over the ocean, I was numb inside. I would pray the same desperate words I had repeated for years: "Lord, please hold me. I'm falling into a dark well." In my journal I wrote, "I feel as if I am disappearing a little more every day. I am so afraid. I feel so alone."

I felt my sanity wavering, unable to find traction. Although I was still functioning on the show, I knew that my distress was beginning to show. One morning as I was listening to a guest I was interviewing answer a question, I found myself staring at her. I didn't have a clue who she was. I couldn't remember what I had asked her or what I should say to her next. Fortunately, I had some notes on my lap, and I quickly referred to them. The floor director must have seen the look of panic on my face because she asked me after the show if I was okay. I said I was fine. I was too embarrassed to admit what had happened. But it shook me to feel so out of control, out of the present, out of my mind. I didn't feel I could talk to anyone about it, so I tried to dismiss it.

A few days after my memory lapse, I started to cry as I was interviewing a guest. It was her kindness that pulled a brick out of the carefully constructed wall around my heart. Instead of answering my first question, she turned the table and asked me how I was doing. It was an innocent, well-intentioned question, but the compassion in her eyes touched a raw place deep inside me until tears made their way past my internal barricade. I could not stop. I wanted to lie down on the studio floor and cry until I had no tears left. Instead, I locked myself in my dressing room until I was sure everyone had gone home.

That summer I received a letter from one of our viewers saying, "I don't know what it is that is causing you so much pain, my dear, but I can see it in your eyes. Please get some help. I am praying for you."

That letter is one of the most precious gifts I have ever received. Somebody noticed. Someone saw beyond the words of encouragement, beyond the smiles, beyond the perfect hair and makeup. Someone heard me. I cried for a long time when I read it. Here was a woman who shared with me that she herself was struggling with cancer, taking time out to pray for me and tell me it was okay to go for help.

I decided to go home to Scotland for a week in September.

My family lived an ocean away, and I missed them very much. I had already scheduled vacation time away from the show, and I booked my flight to Glasgow, knowing that time at home with those who've loved me all my life would quiet the threatening rumble inside.

The Links of the Past

My mother is a strong link in a long line of godly Scottish women. She knew a little of what was happening to me, but I knew I had to try to prepare her for how I looked. I had dropped about twenty pounds, a significant loss on my five-foot-four-inch frame.

Mum had seen bad times herself. When I was five years old, my father had suffered a brain thrombosis that not only changed his ability to live a normal life but also drastically impacted his personality. He died a few months later. His absence was felt every day, but my mother filled our home with her spirit, her faith, and her wonderful sense of humor.

She had always been there for me. When I came home from school, I knew she would be waiting to hear all about my day. When I was eleven, I asked my mother if she would pray with me. I wanted to make a personal commitment to beginning my own journey with God, even though I had no idea where that road would lead.

For a while I wanted to be a missionary in India. I don't think I experienced a specific call to the mission field; it just sounded like the ultimate sacrifice. I hated to be away from home, and I was petrified of snakes and spiders, so I figured such a visible, measurable sign would show God that I loved Him. As a child I perceived that I had lost my father's love, and I was terrified that God might stop loving me too.

During my teenage years I remember watching as a friend

from church rebelled for a time, drinking and partying. The impact that had on me was a fierce commitment to be different. I would walk along the beach after church or youth group meetings and pray out loud, calling on the stars to be my witnesses that I would never let God down, that He could always count on me. That prayer became a theme for my life.

At nineteen, I left Scotland to study at London Bible College. I thought I had arrived in paradise. They say that when you are tired of London, you are tired of life. Well, I was wide-awake. I went to the ballet, the opera, the theater, all on student tickets. My seat might have been far away, but I was right there on that stage—I never missed a note. Though I drank in the atmosphere daily, I never forgot for a moment why I was there: I wanted to know God's purpose for my life. Still seeing the mission field as a woman's "best option," I joined so many mission prayer groups I often had to let someone else pray first to remind me what group I was in. (It's Thursday, it must be Africa!)

I began to see that there was a mission field right on my doorstep. As part of our evangelistic practicum, I would visit other college campuses on the weekends. For me this was much more than a course I needed for credit. Some of my friends and I put a band together, and as I stood in college gymnasiums singing about my relationship with God, I knew I had found what I was created for.

When I graduated, I let the boat for Calcutta sail past, and I joined Youth for Christ as a staff member, traveling across Europe and the United Kingdom, singing and speaking in schools, universities, and churches. *Here am I, a musical evangelist*, I often thought. *Lord, send me wherever You can use me.*

And He did. For the next ten years, I traveled all over the world, gaining an increasingly loyal audience. I released several record albums and served as host for a show called the *Rock*

Gospel Show on Britain's number one television network, the BBC. For the first time ever we had a program featuring contemporary Christian and traditional black gospel music.

I remember how I felt when I read the first review of my debut album. It was a very favorable critique, and I read each line as if the reviewer were talking about someone else, not me. When it sunk in that the article was about me, I pasted the bits that made me feel good onto some of the emptiness in my heart. Later, when it became clear that the BBC show was going to be a success, the British *TV Guide* did a two-page story on "Scottish Girl Makes It Big in London." People began to stop me on the streets and ask for my autograph. I was now the girl on television. This persona was much bigger than me, and I felt a little lost in her shoes.

When I moved to America, my life became much more complicated. I love this country, but I am very disturbed by the way Americans view success, particularly in the church. As I became well-known, especially after I moved to Christian television, I was looked on as a "special" kind of Christian, a cut above the rest. My persona was the perfect place to hide. I didn't have to wonder who I was—everyone knew. Yet, like many successful people, I was miserable on the inside, because I had no real sense of self. It was as if I had lots of beautiful threads but no fabric to hold them together. The more I poured out of myself into others, even as my own well was running dry, the more the real me disappeared. In time, all that was left was a smiling plaster shell.

I was still the same scared little girl who wondered what she had done to make her father hate her toward the end of his life. At least that's how it had seemed to me.

After my father suffered his brain thrombosis, his personality changed overnight. Before he came home from the hospital, my mother explained as best she could to my brother and sister and me that although he was still our dad, he was a little different. He was now paralyzed on the left side and he could no longer speak. But I didn't really care. I just knew that my dad was coming home. I was very much a daddy's girl, and I couldn't wait to have him in our house again.

However, I wasn't prepared for just how different he would be. Dad went from being a warm, fun, kind dad to an angry, unpredictable, violent stranger. It was as if his emotions were reversed—those he loved the most prior to the injury, he seemed to *hate* the most when brain storms shook him. It started in little ways. He would spit in my face or pull a chunk of my hair out. Then it got worse. As a child, I actually feared for my life.

The very last time I ever saw my father alive I was sitting by the fire with the little dog he had given me for Christmas, when I suddenly heard Heidi growl. I had never heard this little dog growl before. I turned, and in that moment, I saw that my father was behind me with his cane over my head. A second was all I had to pull the "weapon" away with my five-year-old might. Shaken, I sat frozen as my dad lay on the floor, roaring like an animal. When my mom, who had been in the kitchen, heard what was happening, she put my sister, brother, and me in a room and called for help. It took four men to restrain my dad before he was taken away to what was then called an asylum. He was thirty-four years old. I never saw him again.

I don't remember how many weeks my father was at the mental institution—my mother never spoke about it until I became an adult. I later learned he escaped one night and was found dead the following morning, caught in the salmon nets in the river behind the hospital.

I was haunted for years, not so much by the noise of that day as by the look of absolute hatred in my father's eyes. For me, throwing myself into serving God was the one place I could hide.

Now it seemed as if my perfect cover had reached its sell-by date and was beginning to fall apart.

Going Home

I looked out of the plane as we circled the green fields outside of Glasgow. I was home.

As I stood in the early-morning chill at the airport, waiting for my suitcase, I drank in the wonderfully comforting sounds and accents that had surrounded me as a child.

I rented a car and drove fifty minutes south to my mother's house in Ayr. I love that drive. The roads wind narrowly along green fields, over hills, past herds of the black-and-white cattle this area is known for, and field after field of white sheep. There is a point in the journey where you can first see the ocean. I look for it every time. When I see it, I know I am almost home. The Ayrshire coastline is so beautiful: sandy beaches, cliff tops that hold the remains of an old castle, seagulls, and salty spray.

I drove up the familiar road and parked outside my mother's gate. I knew she would be watching for me, as she always did, kettle boiling, ready to make that first cup of real tea.

When she saw me, she started to cry. I guess I looked worse than I realized. I had asked her not to tell people what was happening in my life; it still seemed too unbelievable to me that my carefully controlled world was crumbling. What made things more difficult was that I couldn't explain what was wrong with me. If I'd had something that showed up on an X-ray, it would have been easier to rally support, but what do you say when you feel as if you are losing your mind? Over that first cup of tea, Mum said, "If you don't want anyone to know that something's wrong, Sheila, you had better stay home all week, because anyone who knows you will be shocked when they see you."

Mum made all my favorites: minced beef with peas, mashed potatoes, home-baked cakes, and piping hot tea, and I began to eat again. It was so good to be there. Our family pastor, an Irish man, came and spent some time with me and prayed for me. His gentle words and strong prayers were like rain in the desert.

My sister, Frances, and her husband and their two little boys live in Ayr too. One night when I was at their house, David, their older boy, presented me with a chocolate cake he had baked himself. "You look ill, Aunt Sheila," he said. "This will help." I received his lopsided offering with gratitude.

Mum and I walked along the ocean and drove over the hills and talked and talked and talked some more. I admitted my internal struggles. I told her what a failure I felt like. I always thought I was the strong one, the one who would be there for anyone else who was hurting. But now I felt so fragile I couldn't even help myself. But that wasn't how my mother saw me. She hugged me and wept with me. She told me to hold on to the Lord, to take each day as it came, and that she loved me. I would need her words for the days to come.

I had hoped a week at home with my family would be enough to strengthen me for whatever lay ahead. Instead, it made returning to my own home much harder. Being in Scotland with people who had loved me all my life actually made me feel much more vulnerable when I arrived back in Virginia Beach. Instead of feeling stronger, I felt weaker, like a mere whisper of a person.

Desperate, Alone

I quickly returned to my former patterns: I couldn't sleep or eat. I felt overwhelmed by fear. I would spend hours preparing for the next day's show, but no matter how many times I read over the key points for an interview, I couldn't retain the information. Everything disappeared into a dark hole. I would wake up at three o'clock every morning, wide-awake and afraid. Some nights I felt as if I couldn't breathe, and I would lie on my bedroom floor, wishing God would just take me home. "Lord, hold me," I begged. "I'm falling fast."

On the job and over a national grapevine, people were asking or surmising what was wrong with me. I had spent so much of my life measuring who I was by how other people viewed me. Now I was in a time of crisis, and many people wanted to know what was happening to me. How could I explain to people who called from all around the country what I was struggling to understand myself? I thought I was going to drown.

I watched my coworkers watching me. It was obviously very difficult for some of my friends at CBN to know what to say. Many of them simply stayed away. I read their distance as a silent agreement that my life was over.

All sorts of theories circulated around town. Someone had suggested to Pat that perhaps I was bipolar. Or, they speculated, was I simply a pathological liar, inventing all this emotional distress?

I received a few letters from friends telling me to get my act together. I wanted so much to be able to pull myself together, but how do you hold a mountain in place when it is crumbling from the inside? I had sought spiritual help from others and had fasted and prayed, begging God to show me what to do. But every day I would see disapproval and dismissal in the eyes of one more coworker. Why do we do that to each other? Why do we react this way when we don't understand?

It became clear to me that I could not continue as I was. I was worsening each day. I was afraid to drive because sometimes I would lose concentration. At times I would find myself much farther down the road than I thought I should be, with no memory of driving there. It was obvious to me that I wasn't thinking clearly.

All the while, in my purse I kept the precious letter from the woman who asked me to get help. I would pull it out and read it over and over again.

With every ounce of strength I could muster, I finally did reach out for help. Pat Robertson knew a little of my situation and had expressed a desire to help. I sat in the waiting area of his office and wondered what to say to him. I looked at the walls covered in awards and letters of thanks from prominent leaders and organizations he had helped. My heartache seemed to fly in the face of all the hope and joy these walls represented.

Pat opened his office door and asked me to come in. I sat on a sofa beside his desk as he fetched a cup of tea for me. He is a very busy man, and I knew that normally an assistant would do that, but on that day he took the time to make it for me himself. He listened as I tried to explain to him what was happening in my life. He asked me a few questions and told me how sorry he was that things had become so bad. And then he prayed with me. With tears streaming down my face, I listened as he asked the Lord to be close to me. He gave me a hug and told me that his office was always open to me.

Several months before, I had interviewed a doctor who had given me his card at the end of the show, indicating that if I ever needed help, I should call. I had kept his card, and after I left Pat's office, I called his secretary to find out if he could recommend someone in my area. He suggested a doctor whom I already knew and trusted. After talking with this doctor on the phone for a little while, he told me he believed I needed to be hospitalized. He suggested a particular Christian hospital program in Washington, DC.

This advice supported my greatest fear. My father had died as a patient in a psychiatric hospital, and I'd always wondered if I would end my days like him—tormented in my mind, in a place surrounded by strangers.

Yet I knew that the doctor was right; I was beyond self-help. I felt heartsick and terrified. My nightmare was about to become reality. My life was over. The doctor said he would check for the next available opening. I made plans to take a leave of abscence from *The 700 Club*, not knowing if I would ever return.

When I told Pat I wanted to admit myself to a psychiatric unit, he was very kind and fatherly, which is how he has always been with me. He made my decision easier than many others did. I was grateful, but Pat's understanding didn't sit well with everybody, specifically some of the executive staff and his spiritual advisors. When you have a ministry centered on healing and powerful testimonies of lives changed, marriages restored, and people receiving instantaneous miracles, having a cohost who looks like a ghost of her former self and is falling off her chair is a problem. It was clear I was unraveling. I was frail, and inches of concealer couldn't mask the dark circles around my lifeless eyes.

It saddens me as I reflect back that I had so little support. Rather than people moving closer, pressing in to see what was wrong, they drifted farther away. And these weren't just the people I connected with on a professional level; they were those I had considered friends.

My shattering image was televised for the world to see and understandably caused some embarrassment. The whispers behind closed doors evolved from a pressing need for damage control to unsolicited guidance.

The day before I left for the hospital in Washington, DC, one of the higher-ups asked to talk to me. He took me on a walk around the lake at our television headquarters. I was so broken at that point I found it hard to breathe in the fresh air. My eyes fell on tranquil waters glistening in the late-afternoon sun as we walked.

"Sheila," he said, taking long, deliberate strides. "I want to be careful saying what I'm about to say. I know you are very fragile, but just hear me out."

I was quiet and simply nodded.

"Have you considered that there is nothing wrong with you? That this is just an attack of the enemy on our ministry? Think about it. Pat is a godly man surrounded by godly men. And he's been in the ministry for years. If the enemy wants to destroy it, he has to look for the weak link in the chain."

An awkward pause followed. I swallowed hard.

"Sheila, you're the weak link. If people find out you are in a mental institution, if this goes public, it's going to do tremendous harm to the ministry. And I just can't believe this is what you really want."

The tears that I had clenched back broke through with his final words, and I sobbed as I walked. Shaking my head, I stammered, "Of course I don't want that. I love this ministry. But I don't have a choice. I have to do this."

I *didn't* have a choice, whether or not it was true that the devil was using me as his pawn to crush CBN. It was over. I couldn't white-knuckle myself through anymore. I simply could not pull myself together. I hadn't slept in weeks. I had barely eaten. I was having more frequent memory lapses. Just a few days earlier, I had stood in front of the ATM for minutes before I could even remember my PIN.

This man's words stung deeply. I don't think he had a clue of the impact his words had on me. But the fact is, they did. And sadly, I silently agreed with what he said.

Yes, I am the weak link.

I was so tired I could not think anymore, and the idea that

the crisis in my life was going to affect a ministry that meant so much to me was more than I could bear. I felt like a hypocrite. How could I sit on national television every day and tell people that if they put their trust in Christ, everything would be all right when things were far from all right with me?

As the conversation trailed off like a distant memory, absent of any resolution, I left the CBN property and headed home. Rattled by his words, I started to believe I was better-off dead.

I headed home to pack for the hospital, but went to the beach instead. A final visit to a familiar friend.

I parked my car and began to walk barefoot on the stretch of sand that had hugged my footsteps for the last five years. I walked toward the ocean's edge, listening to the roar of waves pounding on the shore and retreating into the dark waters. My mind became a blur as I continued to walk past dry ground and my feet dug into the soft ocean floor, ankles soaked by the icy spray. I wanted to keep walking until I couldn't feel anything at all. I wanted to wash away the darkness that I couldn't quite name but that had engulfed me. I wanted to drown out the gossip, the biting whispers, the unanswered questions, the ministry I was destroying by my desperate need to get help.

I wanted it all to be over.

It seems crazy to think about that night now, but at the time I believed the church would be better-off with a dead Sheila Walsh than a Sheila Walsh in a mental hospital. I played out in my head what would happen. The logistics were pretty straightforward. The network would spin my suicide as a tragic accident. They would arrange a memorial service, complete with a video montage of my greatest ministry moments. A few people would say kind words. The people at the network would support each other and rally around the ministry.

The alternative was me being admitted into a psych ward

and ending a longtime, faithful ministry. It made perfect sense to end my life.

The only thing that stopped me from drowning that evening was reminding myself it was the same way my father had died. I couldn't imagine my mother receiving a phone call that another person she loved had disappeared underwater.

I turned my back on the ocean and went home. I stuck to the original plan and packed my bags.

I'm fine; the sun is shining.
God is in the heavens.
All is well with the world.
I am dying; it is dark.
God, where are You?
Have You forgotten me so quickly?

Chapter 2

How Do You Fix What You Can't Name?

Woe to him whom this world charms from Gospel duty.
Woe to him who seeks to pour oil upon the waters when
God has brewed them into a gale. Woe to him who seeks
to appease rather than to appall. Woe to him whose
good name is more to him than goodness. Woe to him
who, in this world, courts not dishonor! Woe to him
who would not be true, even though to be false were
salvation. Yea, woe to him who, as the great Pilot Paul
has it, while preaching to others is himself a castaway.

—HERMAN MELVILLE, *MOBY DICK*

I don't remember anything about the show that October morning. I simply knew that my suitcase was in my trunk, and when the program was over I would drive out of those familiar gates to an unfamiliar and, to me, terrifying world.

A couple of staff members wanted to drive me to the hospital in Washington, but I was determined to go alone. I was ashamed and afraid, and I did not want anyone to see me walk through those doors that would lock behind me.

I don't remember a lot about the good-byes except for one conversation. I had tried to slip out quietly, but one of my friends stopped me at my car. This woman tried to dissuade me from the journey. "Please, Sheila, don't do this. If you do, God won't be able to use you again. Besides, people trust you. Once the public finds out where you've been, well, your ministry will be over."

"I'm not trying to save my ministry," I told her. "I'm trying to save my life."

Looking back, I think she was genuinely trying to help me, even though her words were misguided. I tried to explain where I was coming from, but my words fell on deaf ears. My desperate plea felt like a repeat of the earlier conversation I had with the man at the lake.

Before I was about to say good-bye, she looked deep in my eyes and said, "You'll never be special again."

The words stung, especially coming from a trusted friend. I looked into her face and told her there was nothing else I could do.

The drive took about three and a half hours. I turned on the radio to an easy-listening station hoping to quiet my mind, but the words of friends and colleagues tumbled over each other.

Over and over in my mind I replayed the haunting statements I'd heard in the last month:

"Do you know the damage you are doing to this ministry?"

"I always knew you would lose it someday."

"You will never be trusted again."

I agonized over what I feared were truths. Maybe these people were right. I started having serious doubts as to whether doctors would be able to help me. If I showed them a broken leg, it made sense to me that they would be able to fix that, but how do you mend a broken spirit or a broken mind? And how do you fix something you can't accurately define in words or even pinpoint?

I'd always thought that if I just tried hard enough, I could make everything all right. I had fasted and prayed for twenty-one days asking God to heal whatever was wrong with me. I had thrown myself even deeper into trying to help others who were hurting, praying that by some sort of spiritual osmosis I would be helped. But I had failed, and look where it was taking me—to a psychiatric hospital. What would become of me there?

Welcome, Sheila

By the time I got to the hospital parking lot, it was dark. All I could see was the low, brick building of the psych ward that was connected to the main hospital.

I sat in my car for an hour, sheltered from the chilly autumn air, safe from the unknown. I knew that once I walked through those front doors, nothing in my life would ever be the same. I wondered how I ever ended up like this. I thought of the house I grew up in, of my brother, Stephen, and sister, Frances, of a simple life in a simple town that now seemed to belong to another world. I thought of a "sturdy lass" who had become a liability to everyone around her.

As I sat there looking for the strength to get out and walk that short distance to my new home for a time, it began to rain. As the drops splashed violently on my windshield, I prayed through my own tears: "Lord, I am so sorry that I have let You down. I am so afraid. I don't even know if I am doing the right thing by being here. It feels like I'm running away, but I don't know where else to go. Please help me."

I got out of the car and stood for a moment watching my breath dissipate in the chill. I opened the trunk and pulled out my suitcase. It seemed very light, and I wondered what I might have packed the night before.

I walked up to the door and pressed the buzzer. It opened, and I walked in. A young nurse took my suitcase and asked me to sit down in the lobby for a few moments. She looked as if she was about my age, dressed in white: clean, clinical, safe.

I looked around. It was very quiet. The lighting was subdued. In one corner of the room, another nurse was trying to comfort a woman who was obviously distressed. I wondered if she was a patient or if she had just dropped off a loved one.

When my nurse came back, she took my blood pressure, commenting it was very low. Then she took a Polaroid picture of me. That felt strange, hardly a moment I wanted to treasure forever. The flash burned my eyes, and for a moment I stood, disoriented. Then she took my temperature and showed me to my room.

It was simple and sparse, a bed, a table, a chair, and a small wardrobe. Everything was neutral and quiet.

"I need to go through your things. It's hospital policy," she said. I wanted her to smile, to say something kind, but she seemed detached. I wondered if this was because she knew what lay ahead of me.

I sat on the edge of the bed and watched as she put items to one side. My hair dryer, my makeup, my belts and panty hose— anything I could use to hurt myself. I told her I had no intention of blow-drying myself to death! She didn't laugh. She asked me if I needed anything and then left for the night, telling me that someone would check on me every fifteen minutes until morning. I realized I was on suicide watch.

I sat there for a while. Alone, numb, and cold. *How is it*

possible that this morning I was on national television, beauti-
fully dressed, part of a respected Christian ministry, and now I
am locked up in a psychiatric ward, not even trusted with a hair
dryer?

I thought about my family. They had all been very supportive of this decision, but I wondered how it made my mother feel
deep down inside. Did it revive old ghosts—my father and his
last days in a bleak hospital when he was beyond Mum's or anyone else's help?

I went to use the bathroom in my room and realized the
door couldn't be locked. My room did not lock either. There was
no space to hide. My private little world was over.

I tried to sleep, but couldn't. I wondered who had slept there
before me and what had happened to them. Had their days here
helped them, or were they more disabled than before?

I remembered a friend saying that when the pain of remain-
ing the same is greater than the pain of change, you'll change.
But who was to say that this would lead to anything better?
When I had prayed that simple prayer of commitment to Christ
as a young girl in Scotland, I never for a moment saw my life
looking like this. I wanted to be a missionary to India, not a
patient in a mental hospital.

I knew I was not going to be able to sleep, so I asked the night
nurse if she could give me something to help. She told me she
had no authorization to give medication. Her next words were
both frightening and comforting: "I'm sorry that you are in so
much pain, Sheila, and it will probably get worse before it gets
better, but you are in a safe place."

I picked up my diary and read the last entry:

Today has been the worst day of my life. I feel so afraid and
so alone. All my life is crumbling, and I am vulnerable and

so tired. What if I can't find my way out of all this pain? It washes over me in great waves. I want to reach out to someone, but I don't know who. I feel as if I am dying, but I am not sick. What if no one believes me? What if I become such a burden that I am simply swept aside? I am afraid that I am losing my mind. God help me.

I thought of the words of Father Marple in *Moby Dick*. I had found them quoted in a book I had read the week before. His words echoed in a repetitive loop in my mind:

Woe to him whom this world charms from Gospel duty. Woe to him who seeks to pour oil upon the waters when God has brewed them into a gale. . . . Woe to him whose good name is more to him than goodness. . . . Yea, woe to him who, as the great Pilot Paul has it, while preaching to others is himself a castaway.

God had brewed my waters into a gale, and there was no calm to be found that night. In the midst of this violent upheaval, I was afraid that I, too, would be a castaway, drowned in waters too deep for me. I knew God was there, but to what depths would He let me sink?

A Welcome Visitor

At three o'clock that morning, I had an encounter with an angel. I had never experienced anything like that before or since, but I have no doubt about what happened that night. I was vaguely aware of who I assumed were nurses or orderlies checking in on me, but I never looked up or paid them any mind. I just sat in the corner of the room with my head on my knees.

This one particular person kept walking toward me until his feet almost touched mine. I looked up. He looked like a doctor perhaps, going off duty. He put something in my hands and turned to leave. It was a stuffed animal, a little lamb, the kind of thing you would give to a child. When he got to the door of my room, he stopped, turned round, and said just one thing—one line that pierced the terrifying darkness. He said, "Sheila, the Shepherd knows where to find you." Then he was gone. There is no doubt in my mind this man was an angel. I was there for a month and never saw him again.

Eventually I fell asleep on the floor until a nurse knocked on my door at 6:00 a.m. to begin my first full day at a psych hospital. I wondered for a moment where I was, and then it all came flooding back. I reached for the lamb to make sure I hadn't dreamt it. It was there. I gazed at myself in the mirror. I looked old and tired. I had no makeup to mask the pain and no desire to hide.

First Day

In search of a cup of coffee (and by the way, they only serve decaffeinated coffee in a psych ward), I followed the sound of voices to the patients' lounge. The warm, familiar buzz of noise sounded inviting, but as I walked into the room, some of the patients stopped talking in the middle of their conversations and stared at me. You could hear a pin drop. Though this was a Christian unit within the hospital, it had never even crossed my mind that I might be recognized. A man in his thirties spoke up. "Are you Sheila Walsh?"

"Yes, I am," I replied.

"The one on television?" he continued.

"Yes."

"What are you doing here?"

"I'm a patient," I said, stating the obvious.

"Yeah, right, sure you are." He rolled his eyes and laughed.

"Well, do you think I'm here to do an interview, dressed in my bathrobe?" I asked him.

One of the other patients nudged him to stop talking and get me a cup of coffee, which he brought back with a large grin on his face. "Sorry," he said sheepishly as he handed me the steaming paper cup. "I always say too much."

The lounge looked comfortable and lived-in. Well-used chairs and a sofa were grouped around a television as if awaiting a favorite show. On the other side of the room were some small coffee tables and chairs. About ten people milled around the lounge, drinking coffee, reading, or writing. I would learn they were my group for the next two weeks.

We would meet a few times a day, led by a therapist, and work through intense emotional and mental exercises. We would share secrets, talk about the things the rest of the world outside of our four walls never knew. We would press into our pain, with gladness, with hesitation, with heartache. I stared numbly at the clock on the wall on the far side of the room. *Tick. Tock. Tick. Tock.* Time moved on. I felt detached, as if I had fallen down a well. Even if I tried to talk, my voice would not carry over the distance.

A frail-looking young woman in a soft pink robe came and sat beside me. She told me her name and that she was here because she had tried to take her own life. "Seems kind of wild now," she said, "but I felt so desperate, and I wanted the pain to stop."

The other patients went downstairs for breakfast, but because I was new, I was not allowed to leave the unit. A young man brought a tray to the lounge, and as I was the only one left in the unit, he gave it to me. I lifted the aluminum lid and saw two very tired eggs staring up at me. I put the lid right back down.

After breakfast the group gathered in a circle for the morning devotions and to check in with one another. One by one they said their names and why they were there.

"I'm Michael, and I'm here because of suicide attempts."

"I'm John, and I'm here because I'm bipolar."

When it came to me, I didn't know what to say. "I'm Sheila, and I don't know why I am here."

A couple of people smiled at me as if they understood.

When everyone had said something, they shared prayer requests and prayed for a fruitful day for each person.

I was taken by one of the nurses for blood tests. I believed the best thing to do was to let them run every kind of test on me. If the rumors were true—that I was bipolar, or that I was a pathological liar—then I certainly needed help. If they weren't, it would be good to have that information confirmed by a professional.

After I had given my thirteenth tube of blood, I had my first appointment with the psychiatrist who would work with me. He asked me a question that seemed strange: "Who are you?"

I knew that there was a right answer, and yet I didn't know what it was. I told him that I was the cohost of *The 700 Club*, that I was a singer, a writer, but I knew I was floundering.

He repeated the question, "Who are you, Sheila?"

My mind went over countless photo shoots and page after page of biographical information, but I knew that this was not what he was looking for. He meant the stuff of life, the fabric of my being, but my life was what I *did*, and I didn't know what else to say.

"I don't know," I said as tears poured down my face.

"I know that, and that is why you are here."

I thought of the morning devotional reading with the other patients:

> *The LORD is my light and my salvation—*
> *whom shall I fear?*
> *The LORD is the stronghold of my life—*
> *of whom shall I be afraid?*
>
> (PSALM 27:17)

And so began one of the greatest, most terrifying adventures of my life: to face the truth about myself, to face my fears, to let everything go, and to trust God in the darkness.

I went out into the little courtyard reserved for patients. I sat by the stream that tumbled over the rocks and wrote in my diary:

> *When greatness seems to vanish*
> *faster than the morning mist—*
> *when purple robes dissolve beneath a touch—*
> *when crowds and cheers*
> *are hushed and stilled*
> *and spotlights turn their faces—*
> *I stand alone, I'm smiling in the dark.*
> *He who would be greatest must be the servant of all.*
> *I hear it now, a softer, truer, call.*

A softer call, "Come to me, all you who are weary and burdened, and I will give you rest" (Matthew 11:28). A truer call, "What does the LORD require of you? To act justly and to love mercy and to walk humbly with your God" (Micah 6:8).

As I sat in the quiet of the courtyard, it seemed as if the volcano had stilled for a moment. I watched a little bird sitting on the bare branch of a tree, singing a few notes to itself. The water rippled softly over the stones. In the peace of that moment, I could almost forget where I was. But I knew that the earth beneath my feet was not yet settled. Over the years, tremendous pressures had built up inside me just as the pressure builds inside a volcano. I could no longer ignore it. Vesuvius had erupted.

Of course, I'll never fail you.
You can count on me.
I'm the one who is always faithful.
I feel my feet are slipping.
I hear them count me out.
I'm lost, faithless. I'll never make it home.

Chapter 3

Hiding in the Shadows

We shall not cease from exploration
And the end of all our exploring
Will be to arrive where we started
And know the place for the first time.

—T. S. Eliot, "Little Gidding"

I slipped easily into the regimented routine of the hospital. Out of bed at 6:00 a.m., breakfast, devotions, individual therapy, and group therapy. After lunch, an art class or more psychological testing and evaluation.

Early in my hospital stay, I was concerned about whether I would live through this nightmare. What's more, I was concerned about what would happen to people who had been in a crisis and who had listened to me on television, people who had prayed with me and made a commitment to change. Would they now throw away any good that had been done, believing that nothing of lasting value could flow through a broken vessel? I was sure that some of the people who had placed me on a very high pedestal would be truly devastated when that pedestal began to crumble. For the moment all that had been shared publicly was that I was taking some time off to rest.

I talked to my doctor about this issue for days. He asked me who I had been holding up as the answer: Sheila Walsh or Jesus Christ? I knew what he was getting at, and I knew that Jesus is the only enduring hope for any of us. But I also knew that privilege brings responsibility. We are called to live in a way that honors God. Somewhere along the road, however, I had crossed the line between pointing to the One who is the answer and feeling an overwhelming burden to *be* the answer.

For fifteen years I had traveled all over the world, singing and speaking. When I thought back on the things I had talked about onstage—the fiery love of God, His grace that holds us when all else fails, His mercy on the broken and the bruised—they were the things I knew God in His goodness wants for us all; they were the things I wanted in my own life. So when someone would ask me to pray for her marriage, I did it with all my heart, knowing that God would be delighted to hear the prayer. If someone wanted prayer to find peace in his life, I gladly prayed with passion that this gift of God would be granted.

Gradually, my life onstage became more real to me than my life offstage. When I began to feel that my life was crumbling, I talked more. I talked louder. I tried to talk what-was-not into being, as if the very act of calling it out would make it a reality for me too. Over the years as cohost of *The 700 Club* I had interviewed those who claimed that struggle and suffering continued because of a lack of faith. I didn't believe that, but now I was questioning everything I believed. I knew that God is the one who calls things that are not into existence, "Who gives life to the dead and calls into being things that were not" (Romans 4:17). But what was my role? What did God expect of me?

In the hospital I received mail from people who knew I had been admitted. They called me a hypocrite. One person sent cassette tapes of talks I had given and copies of articles I had written that he asserted seemed ridiculous in light of where I now was. I had been so outspoken about the love and faithfulness of God in the darkest of nights, and now my own words seemed to mock me. Many more personal indictments followed. Each mail delivery felt like one more nail in my coffin.

It was as if I had taken my two favorite children's stories and lived one while longing for the other.

The Wizard's World

I have always loved the story *The Wizard of Oz*. As a child, I was enchanted when Dorothy's world changed from black-and-white to color. Like all children, I adored the Scarecrow and the Cowardly Lion and the Tin Man, and I wanted my very own Toto. (I also thought that the witch looked suspiciously like the woman who served our school meals and made me eat brussels sprouts!)

All these years later I now saw myself not as Dorothy, but as the little man behind the curtain, who, when the truth is revealed, is no wizard at all. When Dorothy discovers that instead of being a ferocious, larger-than-life wizard, he is just a man, she tells him, "You are a very bad man." To this, he replies, "Oh, no, my dear. I'm a very good man. I'm just a very bad Wizard."

That is how I felt in the hospital; I felt like a very bad wizard.

If the wizard in the story had lived without the bells and

whistles, he could have simply told people that they would find what they were looking for as they continued on their journeys. That is what actually happened anyway. But no one wanted to wait that long. They wanted a miracle right then and there.

Like the wizard, I wanted to be able to make everything better for everyone and secretly hoped that the edges of other people's miracles would touch me. That the grace, peace, and comfort given to others would well over into my own life.

It must have been a huge relief to the wizard when the grand charade was over. The "bad wizard" was actually a very nice man! I felt relief too. It was painful but liberating to have the curtain pulled away. I was finally beginning to understand what freedom looks like. All I wanted now was to be one of the people on the journey.

Something about television makes you larger-than-life, particularly Christian television. Whenever I would bump into viewers in a shopping mall or grocery store, it seemed to me that they believed I had a hotline to heaven, a number that God would pick up before He answered calls from "mere mortals." I'm sure part of it was simply that I was recognizable as a Christian; they knew they could ask me to pray for them. But at times it spilled over into something that scared me.

I remember a man who drove with his very sick wife for ten hours to visit me at the studio because he believed that she would be healed if I would pray for her. It was a privilege to pray for this woman, but why did he have to drive so far when God was with them all along?

I talked with him about that. His answer was simple and, to me, daunting—that God was more likely to listen to me. He confessed he had made too many mistakes in his life and believed he wasn't worthy of an answer. When he looked at me on his television screen, he saw someone with the golden ticket. I tried to explain that none of us deserves an answer, that it is all God's grace, but I don't think he believed me. To him, it sounded too good to be true.

How ironic. It's as if we have taken the truth and made it a fairy tale, and taken a fairy tale and made it the truth. Life would be so much easier if all we had to do was find our way down that yellow brick road to God, and there in the Emerald City, He would grant our every wish. We would bring our fear and our anger and our pain and our sickness to Him, and with a puff of smoke and a thundering voice He would take them all away. There would be no obstacles on the road, no enemies determined to stop us from completing our journey—just a clear, golden path.

The truth is that there *will* be a day when all sorrow and suffering will be dispelled and every tear wiped away, remember?

> Then I saw "a new heaven and a new earth," for the first heaven and the first earth had passed away, and there was no longer any sea. I saw the Holy City, the new Jerusalem, coming down out of heaven from God, prepared as a bride beautifully dressed for her husband. And I heard a loud voice from the throne saying, "Look! God's dwelling place is now among the people, and he will dwell with them. They will be his people, and God himself will be with them and be their God. 'He will wipe every tear from their eyes. There will be no more death' or mourning or crying or pain, for the old order of things has passed away." (Revelation 21:1–4)

That is a promise, but it is a promise of a day to come. How shall we live till then?

That is where my other favorite childhood story comes in.

Loved to Life

Now, this is a glorious story!

If you have never read *The Velveteen Rabbit*, please buy a copy. It is truly a gift. To me, it is a parable of biblical import. When the story begins, the cloth Rabbit is plush and new, stuffed inside a little boy's Christmas stocking. Other new toys come along, ones that *do* things, ones that make noises, and somehow the little Rabbit gets lost in the shuffle.

In the quiet of the night, the toys talk to one another. One toy, the old Skin Horse, is consistently kind to the Rabbit. One day the Rabbit asks him, "What is Real?"

"Real isn't how you are made," says the Skin Horse. "It's a thing that happens to you, when a child loves you for a long time."

The Rabbit asks the Skin Horse if it hurts to become real. The Skin Horse, who is always truthful, says that it does sometimes, but when you are real, you don't mind being hurt. He tells the little Rabbit that becoming real does not generally happen to those who have to be carefully kept. That's because by the time you are real, most of your fur has been loved off. The Rabbit sighs at the thought of what seemed to be such a painful process. I identify with the Rabbit's sigh. If only we could become real without it hurting, without it taking so much time.

The Skin Horse had the wisdom that is born out of time to those who listen to their lives. He had watched all the trends that come and go, but he knew there is no eternity in fashion. When new, he himself had been loved by a little boy, and the marks of that love were etched on the furless patches of his body, his tail hair pulled out to string beads.

Unlike the wizard, the Skin Horse had no bells and whistles, just a calm surrender to the process of life, a deep awareness of what real love looks like. He had spent himself on his master, with no thought for himself, believing this was what he was made for. His shoes were old and worn, but they fit like a glove.

Not so for the wizard. The wizard was meeting a need, a handful of them for that matter, but he was living a lie. When the curtain fell back, it revealed a little old man sweating, huffing, and puffing to maintain the facade. He looked as if he were about to have a heart attack. There was nothing comfortable or natural about his life. The old Skin Horse was far from being the latest thing in the nursery, but he was loved for who he really was. As he said, "When you are Real, you can never be ugly except to people who don't understand."

The message of those two stories was clear to me. I could spend the rest of my life behind the drapes, pulling levers and talking loudly, or I could find out what I was really made for. I wanted so badly to be real. It is one thing to find stories that shed a little light on our paths, but how do we live in the midst of our own stories when it seems as if no good can come of any of it?

After a few days in the hospital, it became clear to me that the Lord had been trying to get my attention for a long time. Books I had read in preparation for my show rang distant bells in my mind. I would read certain pages over and over as I compiled a list of questions for my guests, sensing there was something I needed to understand, but I could never quite grasp what it was.

Now I was in a place where I had the luxury of time. Here I could begin to look at my life. And with that glorious opportunity of self-reflection, of ultimate awareness, came great pain. No one ever said looking in and digging deep would be easy.

It had been a pattern of mine in the past to suppress uncomfortable feelings. I didn't know what else to do with them. So when I was unable or unwilling to deal with what was true about my life, I buried it. I buried the anger I felt at my father's illness and suicide. I buried the hurt from a friend's misguided words. I buried the pain of my first boyfriend's rejection. I buried the humiliation of never being able to afford the "right" clothes to wear. And even though I ended up walking on a lumpy carpet, it had begun to feel normal.

> *Denial is my closest friend—*
> *it keeps the world at bay;*
> *it makes me dance to any tune*
> *and say what I should say;*
> *it builds a wall around my heart*
> *invisible but strong.*
> *I'm always there*
> *but never quite belong.*

But the tide was beginning to turn. I watched as others at the clinic found the courage to deal with things they hated about their lives. *Courage!* What a huge word. It would take me years to understand that courage is a gift from God to make me stronger in Him, not something that might destroy me.

During a group session, our therapist asked this one woman to contribute to that morning's meeting, as she had never yet spoken a word. She stared at him blankly, and he pressed further. Suddenly she lost all control and threw her chair across the room. It bounced off the wall and landed in the middle of our circle as some members of the group frantically scrambled back to avoid getting hit. (It became clear to me that day why we used plastic chairs.)

I was shocked by the rage that shook her. She had seemed so nice, mild, quiet. Apparently I was not the only one who lived on top of a volcano. When she finally calmed down enough to talk, we discovered through her tears that she had been brutally raped as a young girl and had never told anyone. Instead, she had buried the memory and thrown herself into Christian ministry to try and numb the pain. Work more, strive more, feel less.

The group talked together for a long time. One of the younger women shared how she, too, had been devastated by a rape, but buried the pain, as it was caused by a close family member. One by one as a group we gifted one another with the secrets that had terrorized our lives. It felt profoundly holy, like how we as the church should be.

The woman who threw the chair had believed for years that somehow the rape was her fault, and she needed to pay for it. And pay for it she did. She learned that working punishingly hard every day offered a buffer from the anger boiling just below the surface. She didn't have to face what she masked, what she hid, what she covered through constant human effort. The irony, though, was that she knew the power of her stuffed emotion, that if her anger ever escaped, it would consume her. She was sure that if anyone in the Christian organization where she worked found out what had happened to her, they would ask her to leave. To avoid being found out, she had chosen to live in the shadows.

What I saw powerfully enacted before me that day is this: You can try for years to deny the things that are tearing at your soul, but they will not go away. They thrive in the shadowlands, and if you don't deal with them, they will one day deal with you.

No Shadowlands with Christ

My counselor encouraged me to take a deeper look at the way Jesus lived among His friends and the people whose paths He crossed. I took a long look at two different people who were in trouble and had an encounter with Christ: a woman whose life was in chaos, and a man who had no idea what he would become when the pressure of life became intense.

The woman's story is found in John 4:1–42. It was a miracle that Jesus talked to this Samaritan woman at all, for Jews had nothing to do with Samaritans. Not only did Christ talk to her but He also asked her for a drink, which would have been unheard of in those times as a drink from a Samaritan would have contaminated Him according to Jewish law.

This woman knew she was in trouble. I would imagine the distant rumble had become a very familiar sound to her, as it had for me. Relationally, her life was a mess. She had been married five times and was now living with a man who was not her husband. I doubt she had many friends. She would have been mistrusted by women and joked about among men. That's why she was gathering water alone at noon, the hottest point of the day, when she knew she wouldn't have to face those looks and whispered words.

But Jesus looked—really looked—at her and talked to her as if she mattered, because to Him, she did. When John recorded in his gospel that Jesus "*had to* go through Samaria" (John 4:4, emphasis added), the sense there in the Greek is of divine imperative. Christ was on a mission to let one particular broken, shamed woman know that God loved her and there was a better way to live.

Something about that down-reaching gaze connected with her, because the woman came clean with Jesus. She had no need to step out of her shadows into the sunlight for a stranger, but she admitted to Him that the man she was living with was not her husband. Truth is always a turning point. What a gift Christ gave her in letting her know that He was aware of her life situation and her questionable past. He knew everything about her. He *knew* her. If He had offered her living water without this truth, perhaps she would have let His words of life bypass her, thinking, *If you only knew.* But He loved her enough to say, "I know it all, and I still love you." That unfamiliar and glorious gift changed her life so that, even as she was gulping it down, she was running to tell others the good news.

"I know it all, and I still love you." That is the convicting, convincing, liberating truth that comes from an encounter with Christ: all is known; there is no need to pretend anymore. I wrestled with that truth. It's hard to lay aside a mask when it looks just like you, and you have worn it for so long that you can't remember what you look like without it.

The Samaritan was a changed woman after that day. She went from being the village outcast to being the first evangelist to her people. We don't hear any more of her story, but after meeting Jesus, she was fully known and fully loved for the first time in her life. She had looked into the face of God, and He was smiling.

The Skin Horse was content with his bruised and battered exterior because his fur had been loved off by someone who treasured him. The nameless woman whom Jesus met at the well was scarred and bruised, too, but her wounds were in her spirit. Not until she came face-to-face with Christ and grasped hold of His truth, His living water, with every fiber in her being did she catch a glimpse of what she was really made for.

It is much more difficult to deal with the truth about your life when you have no idea that you have feet of clay and it suddenly begins to rain. That's what happened with Jesus' friend Simon Peter.

Peter was a rough, strong, bold, loud, salt-of-the-earth fisherman, the kind of friend you would lean on in a crisis. He was passionately committed to following Christ, wherever that took him. When Jesus began to talk of a different end to

His life than the one Peter had envisioned, Peter was confused and hurt. He could never imagine leaving Jesus, let alone deny knowing Him. Surely their relationship had come too far for that. And yet one night Jesus said Peter would deny Him before morning. In anguish Peter cried out that he would die before letting that happen.

In the hospital, I saw so much of myself in Peter: bold and utterly confident in his own abilities to overcome any obstacle in his way. He *knew* Jesus could count on him. Christ gave Peter a glimpse into the horror that lay just around the corner and let him know that when it was all over, not only would Jesus still love Peter but He also had a job for him to do: "When you have turned back, strengthen your brothers" (Luke 22:32).

I wonder how Peter must have felt the day Jesus was executed for crimes He did not commit. Can you begin to grasp the horror of knowing that, when it counted the most, you were not there for your friend—your Lord?

When I used to read that passage, I didn't see myself in Peter's place. Oh sure, it was very familiar to me as part of the passion story, but I had no real empathy for Peter as a man who had to choke on his own words—until mine came back to mock me. Peter, who with his own lips had denied ever knowing Jesus, just as Jesus said he would. Luke tells us that Peter "went outside and wept bitterly" (Luke 22:62). There was no comforting Peter that night. How could anyone take that pain away? When Christ had needed him most, he had been the one to drive the first nail in. Bitter night turned to morning, another endless day; then the darkness closed in on him again.

It was the first day of a new week when Mary came running down the road, screaming to Peter, "His body is gone. Someone has taken Him. The tomb is empty." As words tumbled over words, Peter was already out the door. It was true. The grave had been robbed, and the body was gone. Later that night, as the disciples cowered in a locked room, out of control, afraid for their own lives, Jesus came and stood among them and said, "Peace be with you!" (John 20:19).

They had thought they would never hear His voice again. Peter had thought he would never hear the word *peace* again. But how could he look Jesus in the eye? After all, Jesus had known that Peter would fail Him, and he had.

But history records that, for Peter, life was not over yet. John 21 tells the following story: One morning more than a week later, the fishermen disciples met Jesus for the third time since His resurrection; He sat with them on the beach, cooking breakfast. When they had finished eating, Jesus turned and looked at Peter. "Simon, son of John, do you love me more than these?" Here Jesus used the word *agape* for love. *Agape* is the very nature of God, for God is love.

Peter said yes, he loved Him with *phileo* love. Phileo refers to a strong liking or a strong friendship.

Jesus asked him the question again, "Peter, do you *agape* me?"

Peter again said, "Yes, Lord, I *phileo* you." Jesus asked for a third time, and this time He asked, "Peter, do you *phileo* me?"

A great pause. A moment of truth.

Peter looked at Jesus, I imagine with deep pain in his eyes, and responded, "Yes, Lord, I *phileo* you." *Lord, You know all things; You know that I love You, but this is all I have at the moment.*

And to Jesus, it was enough.

To me, this is one of the most honest, confrontational, liberating dialogues recorded anywhere. Peter's reveal resonated with me. I saw myself standing before Christ, kicking the desert sand with my dirty sandals, looking with longing into the eyes of Jesus. *You knew that I would fail You, even when I talked louder than anyone else. You knew that I am not as strong as I thought I was. So if You knew all that, Lord, You know my heart is broken now, and You know that I love You.*

Peter was given a second chance. He went on to become a martyr of the early church, and as the early church father Tertullian wrote, "The blood of the martyrs is the seed of the Church." Peter's life and death fed the church, for from that life-changing confrontation with Christ on the beach, he was a different man, a man who selflessly gave himself to the building up of the body of Christ. "You are Peter, and on this rock I will build my church" (Matthew 16:18).

> *"O God, I am only dust," I cry*
> *and God picks up the dust*
> *and breathes His life once more.*

Sometimes I think we misinterpret faith. In my own life, instead of grabbing hold of the pain, the mystery, the questions and dealing with it all, no matter how painful, I acted as if everything were fine. I thought if I just *believed* enough, then everything would be all right. But was I living by faith or by wishful thinking? Jesus never encouraged His friends to cover over the pain in their lives, but to bring it into the light, where healing is found. Sometimes we don't do that because we fear being rejected by others. Yes, rejection may well happen, but bringing the pain to the light is still the best way to live. It will take much courage, but it will bring freedom.

Sometimes we simply don't want to face the truth about ourselves; the myth reads so much better. Sometimes we do not seek help because it will mean we have to change, and change is painful and unpredictable. To me, now, faith is bringing all that is true about our lives into the blinding light of God's grace. It is believing that He will still be there at the end of the journey. And so will we, perhaps a little bloodied, probably with a limp, and possibly, as the Skin Horse said, with most of our hair loved off, but we will be there.

Just As I Am

On the second Sunday I was in the hospital, I had permission to go to church with a nurse and eight other patients. I let the singing of those glorious hymns wash over me as we sat in the back row. Sunlight streamed through the stained glass, bringing it to life. The pastor spoke about those of us who feel we have failed God in our mission on this earth. I felt he was speaking directly to me. I looked at the nurse out of the corner of my eye, wondering if she had had a word with him before the service, but in my heart I knew it was the Lord. I felt as if God's presence had invaded every corner of the sanctuary. I couldn't lift my head. It was as if I were on holy ground.

The pastor concluded the sermon with an illustration. "There are some of you here today who feel like dead people. It is as if you are already six feet under, staring up at the top of your own locked coffin. This morning Jesus wants to set you free. You simply have to let go of the key and pass it through the little hole, where you see a tiny shaft of light."

I listened as if I were the only person in the room. I had never gone forward to an altar before; I had prayed to be accepted into God's family in my bedroom. I asked the nurse if it would be all right if I spent a few moments at the altar, and she said yes. I ran down the aisle that day. Yes, I ran. I did not care who saw me or what they thought. All I knew was that I was dying and someone was telling me where to get help.

I lay facedown at the front of the church with the words of

a classic hymn, "Rock of Ages," that my grandmother used to sing to me as a child running through my mind. These two lines became my prayer:

> *Nothing in my hands I bring*
> *Simply to Thy cross I cling.*

I confessed my utter hopelessness and helplessness to Christ and asked Him to forgive me. At one point, I felt compelled to look up. As I did, it was as if Jesus Himself were standing before me with outstretched arms, saying, "Welcome home, child, welcome home."

I stayed there for a while, basking in the radiant forgiveness being lavished upon me. It was one of the most beautifully humbling moments of my life. A gift had been given that would never be taken from me. I knew this to be true because I had done absolutely nothing to earn it, and it was given to me in my most unlovable hour.

That afternoon a group of us was taken to a supermarket and given thirty minutes to shop. Supermarkets usually drive me nuts because there are so many things to choose from, but I didn't feel that way this time. I walked over to the fresh produce section and looked at the different kinds of apples. Everything seemed so wonderful! It was as if I had never been alive before. I wanted to hug myself, I felt so free.

I was beginning to understand a profoundly simple truth—I am not the good news, Jesus is. When Christ confronted me with this, His words were the strongest and yet the most loving I would hear. They would give me the courage to face the next part of the journey.

Gracious Father,
You know us so well.
You love us so completely.
Forgive us, we pray,
for hiding in the shadows.
Give us the courage to live in the light,
for You are Light,
and You are Truth,
and we are Your children.
Amen.

A winter landscape
no relief
a cold gray blanket
settles on my soul.

Chapter 4

Winter

I am in that temper that if I were under water
I would scarcely kick to come to the top.

—JOHN KEATS

S cotland is known for its beautiful scenery. When the sun shines, there is no better place to be on this earth. The trouble is that it does not shine very often! On the West Coast where my family lives, there are a lot of what we call drizzly days—the sky is gray and heavy, the wind is bitingly cold, and the rain falls down gentle and light, but steady. It feels like a cold, damp blanket wrapped around your shoulders. People hurry home from town, from church, eager to throw off their raincoats and boots and gather by a roaring fire, where the misery of the elements can be consumed by crackling flames.

As a little girl, I liked winter in Scotland. It was quiet, and the sea could finally be heard, since the tourists had all gone home. I would come home from school, take off my navy-and-gold blazer, pull on some jeans and a warm sweater, and head down to the ocean. I would sit there for a long time, enjoying the songs of the sea. Sometimes I would settle onto a rock, close enough to get splashed by the salty spray. I loved it. That was where I did my "serious" praying.

Out there, surrounded by the wind and the water, I knew I served an awesome God. This was no sideshow; this was a tiny glimpse of the splendor of the Lord of heaven and earth. I am basically melancholy at heart and those winter days are part of who I am—a winter person. I love the reds and the yellows of the world, the brighter side, but there will always be a place in my heart for the grays and ebony shades of life.

But my breakdown was different. There was nothing comforting or familiar about any of it. A volcano is a splendid sight, but when it is over, everything around it is desolate, covered in white ash—a silent, winter landscape.

Before I went to the psychiatric hospital, I felt sad most of the time, and tired, but I didn't know why. It was as though winter had settled on my heart with no hope of spring. One of our camera operators said to me one day that I seemed depressed, but I didn't know what that meant. I remembered years before when I was touring in England, the subject of depression had come up. I was on the road with another artist and my band, and a few of us sat down one evening after the concert to eat. Someone said, "Did you hear about Dave?"

A few snippets of information were tossed into the arena, and then someone said, "He has been diagnosed with clinical depression."

The general response of those at the table that night was complete disbelief, and the cynical and sneering comments began to circulate. I know we British tend to favor a stiff upper lip, sometimes minimizing the reality of emotional pain, but the general consensus of opinion that evening was that there is no such thing as depression.

"He just needs to pull himself together, that's all."

"We all have bad days; you just can't give in to them."

"I've always thought he was a bit lazy."

I remember arguing with them because I knew this man, and it made no sense to me that he would pretend to be in so much pain. But the subject soon changed, and I didn't give it much more thought. All I knew was that my friend was sad, and I understood that.

I would eventually come to understand a lot more about depression and how a human heart can ache to the point of breaking.

> *Nothing is what it seems.*
> *I reach for you but you are not there.*
> *I cry for help and you are all around,*
> *keeping me contained*
> *safe and cold within a Hall of Mirrors.*
> *I tell myself that this is the real world,*
> *but my head aches*
> *and my heart aches*
> *and I know this is a lie.*

If you are on a speeding train that is out of control, and you know that you are losing your hold, what do you do? Do you wait till it hits the wall, or do you jump off? I decided to jump. I knew I would be hurt, but I didn't care anymore. I had let things get to a place where I could no longer function.

After a couple of days of medical tests in the hospital, I met with the chief psychiatrist to review the results and find out what was wrong with me. He seemed kind and easy to talk to. He had a strong sense of humor, which I imagined served him well in his chosen profession. He told me he saw no signs of bipolar disease but that I was severely clinically depressed. I exhibited the classic signs: insomnia, loss of appetite, overwhelming feelings of hopelessness, loss of memory, inability to concentrate, loss of emotional control, acute anxiety, and an enduring, unbearable sadness.

The Centers for Disease Control (CDC) says that one in five Americans is being treated for depression and anxiety. The numbers must be far greater when you take into account those who never come forward for help. One of the greatest challenges to those who suffer with this disease is that many people do not believe it is a legitimate illness. I can assure you, it is.

The doctor explained more about clinical depression. It has many contributing factors, he told me, some of which can be physiological. Within the brain there are chemical messengers called neurotransmitters. When these neurotransmitters are at healthy, normal levels, we are able to function well. But the lack of one or more of three chemical transmitters—serotonin, norepinephrine, and dopamine—can be a key contributor to depression. He continued to say my brain needed help in replacing those levels, which were very low. He advised me to take a drug called Zoloft for a while.

I was resistant to the idea of medication for three reasons. First, as a Christian dealing with an emotional and mental crisis, I was skeptical about the wisdom of resorting to pills. Surely I could get through this crisis without them. The cumulative words of so many of our guests on *The 700 Club* came back to me: *If I had enough faith, would I be in this place at all?*

Second, I also believed that God was asking me to look at my life and take responsibility for where I found myself. I believed I needed to feel whatever pain was necessary in order to finally come to grips with my life. I did not want a "feel good" pill to dull the edges.

My third concern was the fear that I would end up walking around with a vacant look in my eyes, drooling on a ratty bathrobe and being followed by my imaginary dog, with whom I would be carrying on a constant dialogue! If there was any chance of this happening, I wanted no part of a drug treatment.

My doctor alleviated my fears. Zoloft, he said, is what they call a serotonin reuptake inhibitor, which would slow down the rate at which my body was using up that valuable messenger. Though it does not solve underlying issues that need to be dealt with, it does give a physical boost—when you see the possibility of spring, you have more strength to walk through the weeks till its arrival. He assured me that this was not a "feel good" pill; that's what they were selling on street corners!

I took the medication, and within a few days I could already tell a difference. Rather than numb me to the things that I needed to deal with, it helped me regain my balance and made me better able to face the long road ahead. Each morning, as I lined up with my fellow patients, I took that little blue pill with a prayer of thanksgiving. (As I write, it is 2014, and I am still on medication. While I tried to wean myself off on two occasions— more on that later—I have made peace with the fact that I will probably need to take it for the rest of my life.)

Among Friends

Many of my new friends whose diagnoses were the same as mine were highly motivated, disciplined people—doctors, pastors, students—who, like me, in the midst of their apparent success, felt the walls were closing in on them. Each of us could have echoed the words of Abraham Lincoln when he said:

I am now the most miserable man living. If what I feel were equally distributed to the whole human family, there would not be one cheerful face on earth. Whether I shall ever be better I can not tell. I awfully forebode that I shall not. To remain as I am is impossible, I must die or be better, it appears to me.

Lincoln struggled with depression for most of his adult life. I wonder if anyone understood what was happening to him and stood beside him, or did he have to walk alone? In the midst of this gray, winter landscape, one thing was clear to me: I was not alone. There was a nail-scarred figure walking with me through the snow.

> When I said, "My foot is slipping,"
>   your unfailing love, LORD, supported me.
> When anxiety was great within me,
>   your consolation brought me joy.
>   (PSALM 94:18–19)

In the hospital, God gave me—and other patients—clear signs that we were not suffering in solitude. I'll never forget one encounter. I had been there for a couple of weeks and felt pretty much at home. After dinner one evening, I was wandering through the lobby to go to my room when I became aware of a family entering the hospital. What I assumed were two daughters were gently propping up their crying and moaning mother, supporting her as she shuffled beside them.

As they got closer to the front desk, I recognized the look of despair in the mother's eyes. Not wanting to stare, I began to turn around to give this family some privacy. Then the strangest thing happened. The mother looked up at me, let out a cry, and threw her arms around me. I was taken aback. Gripped in this woman's embrace, I immediately looked around for her daughters to see if they were going to attempt to pry their mother from this stranger. But when they saw what was happening, they, too, began to cry.

I was a little bemused. I wanted to be welcoming, but I was exceeding my own expectations! Eventually one of the daughters pulled herself together enough to give me some background. Their mother had lived for forty years with their father, who brutally beat her. Her children had tried to persuade her to leave him many times, but as a Christian she wanted to honor the vows she had made to God all those years ago. She had finally left after one terrible beating, but was so overwhelmed with guilt and fear that she had settled into a deep depression. Her daughters were very concerned about her and had spent a long time trying to persuade her to get some help. They could see she was sinking fast, but she was very afraid and ashamed of being admitted to a psychiatric hospital.

As they drove to DC, they prayed that the Lord would give her a sign as she walked through the door—a sign that she was in a safe place. That's where I came in. She had watched me on television every day and saw me as another daughter. When I was there, walking through the lobby in my pajamas, clearly a patient and not a visitor, she and her daughters saw me as the "sign." Isn't that just like the Lord? He cared for this dear woman so much that He placed us there together, at just the right moment.

Weeping with Those Who Weep

Every day brought fresh questions to the surface. One of the questions I continued to wrestle with in the hospital was, "What is real faith?" I believe it will always be God's will to restore families, to mend broken lives so that we can continue to journey together. I hold that truth close to my heart as I walk in a broken, fallen world.

What I think we as the church lack, though, is a place to talk about how things really are right now. In our desire to be an inspiration to one another we often veil what is true, because what is true is not always inspirational. It's not easy to watch or personally experience a marriage on the verge of divorce, or a child battling cancer, or a betrayal of the worst kind, or dreams lost in the dust, or overwhelming feelings of despair or emptiness. But these things are real. And hurting believers whose lives are in tatters need real help. If we were able to put aside our need for approval long enough to be authentic, then, surely, we would be living as the church.

Sometimes we encourage one another to live inauthentic lives. My mother once told me a story from when she was dating my father. They twice visited a new church that placed great emphasis on praising God in the midst of trials. This is obviously a scriptural mandate, so who could fault them?

At one particular meeting, a young woman who had just lost a baby stood up and gave thanks for the trials in her life, giving glory to the Lord, saying that in Him there is no need to grieve and we can continue to march on victoriously. My mother was horrified by this woman's seeming indifference to the loss of her child, but the rest of the congregation clapped in approval of her apparent great faith. After the service ended, my mom heard someone in the bathroom weeping bitterly in one of the cubicles. It was the mother, who, having done the "right thing," was now expressing her genuine emotions all alone in a dark place.

It makes me so angry to think that someone in such terrible pain had to weep alone. Perhaps you think this story sounds extreme, but versions of it are played out every day in our evangelical communities. We all experience loss at some point in our lives, whether it be the loss of a marriage, a career, a loved one, or a dream, and too often we are disapproved of by others who are insensitive or oblivious to our pain.

I remember a colleague who was diagnosed with cancer. He was married and had children who needed their daddy around. The staff made plans to gather around him and pray for his healing. After we had finished, the man leading the prayer time said, "Go and walk in your healing." I'm not quite sure what that meant, but there seemed to be a general consensus that everything was all right now.

Several months later the man died. The funeral came and went. None of us on staff, particularly those who prayed in the chapel that day, said a word. Life carried on as usual. There seemed to be no accountability to our words at all, just a faint embarrassment and the unspoken indictment that there must have been something else about the man we did not know. Perhaps he harbored some unconfessed resentment in his heart, or a sin of the past was still tied round his leg like a millstone. When I think back to that time and the way we all handled that delicate matter, the man who died seemed to be the only one who was not afraid.

Living Honestly

When we don't deal honestly with our lives and the losses we face, when we try to anesthetize the pain and move on, then the suppressed anger or fear or guilt will deal with us until we are ready to deal with those issues.

When the Israelites were carried off into captivity in Babylon, Psalm 137 says they sat down by the river and wept. Jeremiah records the despondency that lay upon the people as they remembered their homeland. They had lost their homes;

they had lost their joy. God was still on the throne but His people were in pain, and they wept that pain out.

I wonder sometimes if we think it ungodly to mourn the changing seasons of life, as if doing so were to question God's wisdom. I do not believe that expressing the pain we feel diminishes God or our faith in Him. Everything in our lives comes to us through the gracious hands of the Lord, but that does not mean our lives will be free of pain. In fact, we are told that life will include hurt and hard times.

> *A time to kill and a time to heal,*
> *a time to tear down and a time to build,*
> *a time to weep and a time to laugh,*
> *a time to mourn and a time to dance.*
> (ECCLESIASTES 3:3–4)

If we do not tear down, we can never lastingly build. If we do not take time to mourn, we will have no joy in dancing, and if we do not fall down on our faces at times and weep, we will never be swept away with laughter. Jesus said, "Blessed are you who weep now, for you will laugh" (Luke 6:21). Ironically, we seem to have a love affair with the lighter side of life, as if any intensity of emotion would consume us.

Perhaps, too, in the "shift-the-blame" society we live in, we have forgotten how to weep over our sins. David, the psalm writer, said, "When I kept silent, my bones wasted away through my groaning all day long" (Psalm 32:3). I wonder if so many of us rush off to self-help groups because we have lost the ability to be real in our churches.

Lately, many articles written in fundamentalist circles have warned against seeking psychological and psychiatric help, describing them as tools of Satan. It is true that among the tidal wave of pop psychology and self-help manuals there have been many that have served to further debilitate, but someone who is ill does need help. I have no time for programs that encourage us to pass the blame to others, but it is my experience that there *can* be tremendous value in taking a long, hard look at our lives, understanding some of the reasons we made the choices we made, making peace with the past and moving beyond the past, beyond the winter to spring.

I now think it takes more faith to name our need than to keep *believing* that something will happen and not doing anything about it. It takes faith, and great courage, to get help, to take the first painful step toward the dream that is in our hearts. I have stood before crowds and delivered passionate messages on what I believed was possible in my own personal life, but I know now that you can look at bricks and cement for years, believing in the vision of a home, but until you get down on your hands and knees and start to build, it will remain a dream.

There is today still an incredible stigma attached to any mental illness, whether depression, anxiety or panic disorders, to name a few. Countless people have told me that they suffered silently for years, afraid to tell anyone how they were feeling. No intelligent person would condemn someone for having a brain tumor, so why do many people discount or distance themselves from a different form of trouble? What is, is. Depression will not go away by pretending that it does not exist.

While I was in the hospital, I was very shaken when a pastor and his wife telephoned one evening and encouraged me to leave the hospital; they believed that a Christian shouldn't be in a "place like that." I later learned that one individual in our group had violated the code of confidence and telephoned her sister to let her know that I was a patient. Her sister in turn had telephoned her pastor, and I was now being challenged by two complete strangers. I have heard various other attempts—some that seem contradictory to others—to rationalize depression and other mental illnesses in the church:

- "It is a punishment from God."
- "To seek help is to doubt God's ability to heal."
- "If we suffer enough, God will be pleased."
- "It is a spiritual illness that should only be treated by God's personal intervention."

I can't tell you how many people I've spoken with over the years whose loved ones committed suicide because no one understood the agony of the journey they were on. No one took time to ask or hear about their pain. Their hurt. Their fear. Their shadows. Their dark places. Their tormenting thoughts. They were simply dismissed as irrational or weak.

Some years ago I met a woman in her sixties. She pulled out a worn photograph of a beautiful young lady in her mid-twenties flashing a million-dollar smile and cheery eyes. "This is my daughter," the woman told me with lips quivering. "She was on staff at a large, well-known church and struggled with depression. She had asked to take a short leave to seek psychiatric help and get on necessary medication." The woman shook her head and paused to compose herself. "They told her no. That they didn't believe in that, but would pray for her."

This woman's daughter committed suicide not long after.

Hearing stories like this makes me sad and angry. I'm sure this young woman was shamed into thinking there was something wrong with her, just as I was. That because she was a woman, she was probably too "emotional." This young woman did not have to die. She—and others before and after her—did not have to get to the point of utter hopelessness where they believed the only chance of escape was suicide. Mental illness is a treatable disease. It exists. It is real.

Permission to Get Help

My doctor encouraged me to face the truth about my life: to stop running, to stop making excuses, to step up to the plate and take responsibility for my own life. He also helped me understand that mental illness is a reality, a treatable reality, and there is no shame there. The lack is not in faith but in brain chemicals.

We all need to come to a point when we will take responsibility for our choices and our healing. If you are struggling alone, sinking a little more every day, I would encourage you to get help. Depression, like many other mental disorders, is a treatable illness, and there is no shame in reaching out for help. In fact, it takes a lot of courage to take that step.

But depression is also only one of the ways we are alerted to trouble inside of us. Some people drink to forget; this, and other addictions or things we use to distract or numb ourselves (like compulsive shopping, watching mindless TV for hours, filling up our social calendar to avoid the quiet), treat the surface problem, but they don't make the underlying problem go away.

Other people are alerted by a general disquiet in their souls, a haunting rumble that says all is not well. If the trouble is in a marriage, too often people wait to get help only when both partners are "ready." While this is obviously the ideal scenario, it may not happen that way. You can choose health for only one person: yourself. Yet so often people wait and wait as their lives crumble a little more every day. It takes courage to ask for help, but only by asking will we find the help we need.

I know that those daughters I met in the hospital would have given anything to encourage their mother to seek help sooner, but once she finally did it, they stood by her every day and lovingly reminded her that she wasn't crazy or spiritually lost or "less than." She just needed to work through the aftermath of being abused and beaten by her husband for years. They spoke what was true to her, no matter how heartbreaking the truth was.

One day we will all stand alone and answer to God for the choices we have made in our lives. It will not be enough to say we did not get help because no one would come with us. Life is not easy, but we make it much more difficult when we refuse to be honest about what we feel. For the short term, not being honest may seem easier, but in the long haul, we pay a heavy price.

When I decided to get some help with my life, I had no idea where that path would take me. All I knew and held on to daily was that Jesus loved me. As I began to uncover some painful issues, I felt as if my heart were being ripped out of my body. But I still knew that Jesus loved me. We have this fact to hold on to in the darkest nights of our lives. It will never change. It will always be true. Yes, Jesus loves me!

Most often what holds us back from being honest is fear. I have discovered that glass cages may look nice, but they are no place to live.

> *One day I decide to see if there is more*
> *beyond these mocking, mirrored walls;*
> *there is only one way out:*
> *It is through the glass.*
> *I cut my hands, my feet, my heart.*
> *I think I'll bleed to death,*
> *but the ground I am on is solid,*
> *though covered with my blood.*
> *I look over my shoulder*

to see my glassy cage,
but it's not there.
It was only an illusion,
an illusion strong enough to make me bleed.

If you are struggling to try and help someone who is dealing with depression, don't worry about saying the right thing, just *be there*. The ministry of presence is a beautiful gift to take to a sickbed. There is also something so healing about touch. Scripture illustrates the power of the laying on of hands.

"It happened that the father of Publius lay sick with fever and dysentery. And Paul visited him and prayed, and putting his hands on him healed him" (Acts 28:8 ESV).

"Therefore let us leave the elementary doctrine of Christ and go on to maturity, not laying again a foundation of repentance from dead works and of faith toward God, and of instruction about washings, the laying on of hands, the resurrection of the dead, and eternal judgment" (Hebrews 6:1–2 ESV).

I know it can be difficult to deal with something that seems to take so long to lift. Winter is a cold, harsh season that offers little comfort or shelter. It is a bleak and weary landscape, but underneath that heavy blanket, like the drizzly days of a Scottish winter, there is life, new life; it just takes time. As I understand God's Word, it is not the pace of the race that matters, but that we all finish together.

It's like a story a friend once told me. He was watching the Special Olympics on television. During the course of one of the races, a boy with Down syndrome fell facedown onto the track. There was a gasp from the crowd as they watched the boy's dreams being dashed on the merciless tarmac. Suddenly all the other runners stopped, went back, and picked him up, and they crossed the finish line together.

We have much to learn from those we see as disadvantaged. There are many people in the church who live under the weight of depression as if it were a broken arm that may well heal if left alone. But "leaving it alone" is not the solution. I discovered that depression was not the core of my problem. Although it is a very real illness that needs to be treated, it's the rumblings *inside* the volcano that cause the eruption. For me, depression was my struggle. It was the flag that was trying to get my attention. I would be shocked by what it showed me.

> *Lord, it is dark.*
> *I can't see the path ahead of me.*
> *You are the light of the world,*
> *and so I ask that You would show me the way.*
> *I have trusted You in the daylight.*
> *I trust You now in the night.*
> *Amen.*

Part 2

The Valley

Today I am afraid.
My enemies are many;
they march up to my door
and blow with all their might.
They take my name and tar and feather it
for all the world to see.
I stand and watch.
They whisper in my ear,
"It's all over.
The curtain's coming down.
The crowd is going home.
The lights are going out."

Chapter 5

Why Are You Afraid?

To live with fear and not be afraid
is the final test of maturity.

—EDWARD WEEKS

I magine with me for a moment overhearing a dialogue occurring in the throne room of heaven between the Father, Son, and Holy Spirit. The subject of the debate is how to answer Sheila Walsh's prayer.

"She says she is tired of being afraid. Perhaps we could give her the gift of courage."

"It might be a finer gift to remove all the things that she is afraid of."

"We could always bring her home if it becomes too much for her."

A strong, quiet voice speaks up. "No. We will invite her greatest fears to visit her. They will take up residence, but only for a while. It is only in living with them that she will ever overcome them."

That is how it seemed to me. It was as if everything I have ever been afraid of decided to take center stage in my life.

Fear felt like a physical illness to me. It was as though it had a stranglehold on my heart and mind. It made me literally, physically sick. It is one thing to be afraid of the school bully or to have nightmares as a child or to hate the dark, but it is another thing when we carry those fears into our adult lives and allow them to dictate how we should live.

The Tests Reveal . . .

Let me take you back to my first morning in the hospital. After they had taken my blood, I went through hours of psychological testing. I was extremely tired and found it hard to think, but perhaps that was the best scenario because I couldn't work out what would be the right answer; I could only say what came to my mind. The doctor held up pictures and asked me to tell the story behind the scene. I answered question after question till my head ached. Finally, at eight o'clock at night, the testing was finished.

A few days later that same doctor called me into his office to discuss the results. "The tests indicate that you are very angry and sad inside, Sheila, but you never give yourself permission to feel the anger or to speak up for yourself. You need people to approve of you. You allow fear to make many of your choices. It is as if there is a huge, empty place inside of you, but you don't let anyone in. How does that sound to you?"

I started to smile. I'd been there less than a week, but it had already become a joke among the other patients that I followed every rule and did everything right. I was even the first in line every morning to get my medication! But the smile quickly faded.

His words made me sad because they rang so true. Fear, anger, need for approval, loneliness—all were deeply rooted in

me, and I would soon come to see that they were all closely connected and major factors in my depression.

The doctor asked me what I was so afraid of.

I gave him one answer: I was afraid of losing what defined
me; I was afraid that if you took away all the fancy wrapping of
my life and looked inside the box, it would be empty.

But that answer led to others. I was very afraid of certain
types of people, not because I wanted to win their approval, but
because I believed they could wipe me away if they decided to.
If I had to deal with an aggressive, driven personality who was
easily angered, for instance, I would dance around that person
mentally, taking their temperature to make sure they would not
blow. I couldn't see that someone could be very angry with me
and say what was on their mind without destroying me in the
process. At the deepest level, I feared for my survival. My life
was like a tightrope, where balance was everything, and if I lost
concentration for even a moment, all would be lost.

I was also afraid of anger itself. I remember, when I was about
twenty years old, spending a day in Glasgow with my brother. We
were walking down one of the busiest streets in the city when a
man came up to Stephen and gave him a pen. It was a basic con,
the principle being that once you actually have the pen in your
hand, you "owe" the man some money.

My brother had had this happen to him a few times before,
and he decided enough was enough. He was going to keep the
pen and move on. The man followed us, getting very angry and
yelling at Stephen to give back the pen, but my brother ignored
him. The minute this man raised his voice, something snapped
inside me. Fear tore through my being. I began to cry and begged
my brother to give the pen back to this stranger. Seeing my obvious distress, he quickly did so.

I couldn't explain to Stephen why I had reacted in such an

intense way. I only knew that when I was around anger or angry people, I feared for my survival.

First Fears

I had always had some understanding of why I was afraid of anger. But with the doctor and later with my mother, I was able to revisit and walk through a painful, devastating period of my childhood—the year of my father's illness. One of the things that was most healing to me was my mum's presence. In my first two weeks of inpatient treatment, I worked with the doctor alone. But later, in the second phase of my treatment when I had moved into a hotel and came to the hospital each day for treatment, my mother came to be with me.

Without my even asking, she flew over from Scotland and stayed for a month. I will be eternally grateful that I have a mother who has always made it easier for me to believe that God's love will never fail me, because her love never has. I know it was painful for her to sit in sessions with me and relive what were the hardest days of her life, but she did it unquestioningly because she knew it helped me.

When I look at pictures of me as a little girl before my father's illness, my eyes are full of mischief. As a preschool child, I was a tomboy, fearless and full of life. My mother declares that she didn't get to sit down till I was five years old. As a child I adored my father. He understood my tomboy ways and gave me space to fly. At this stage of my life, anything seemed possible. After my father's death, I was not so sure.

After he was taken away to the asylum the terrible day after he tried to hit me with his cane, I never saw my father again. Children didn't go to funerals in those days in Scotland. I just remember my mum coming home one day in a black dress and a black hat, and we never talked about him again. All his photos disappeared into a suitcase under my mother's bed. I had to come to my own conclusion as to what happened and determined his death was my fault. I carried that lie and, as a result, a tremendous amount of guilt with me everywhere I went.

Because of me, a wife had lost her husband. A child, my baby brother, would grow up without a father, and my sister would have no one to walk her down the aisle when she got married. I had to make things right somehow. And boy, did I try. For years, I would buy my little brother all the things I thought my dad would have given him—toy cars and trains, books. I shouldered the same guilt with my mother. It bothered me that no one bought her nice gifts like a husband would. I remember being twelve years old and packing most of my treasured possessions, including my favorite dolls, into a suitcase to sell to my fellow classmates during lunchtime. I wanted to give her what she didn't have.

My father's death devastated me. I was too young to understand what had happened to him. All I knew was that at the end he seemed to be very angry with me, and then he was gone.

I'm sure my mum thought that if I wanted to talk about my father's death, I would, but she could have no way of understanding the conversation that was going on inside my head. I was left with a question that no one on earth could answer. *What did my father see in me that made him hate me so much?*

Children are the best recorders of information—they miss nothing; but they are the poorest interpreters.

As adults we understand how the brain can be ravaged, changing a personality, but a child has no capacity for medical diagnosis or such logic. With the information I had as a five-year-old, I came to a wrong conclusion about my life: I must have done something to make my father so angry. I was determined that no one would ever again be angry with me. I became a very good girl who never rocked the boat.

When I gave my life to Christ as an eleven-year-old, I was

overwhelmed by the love and acceptance I felt from God. It became my life's work to never lose that love. But I always wondered, *If those closest to you can change their minds, would it be possible to do something to lose the love of Jesus too?* I had no idea what I had done to change my dad, so how would I know what would make God look away? As I matured as a believer, I came to know that it was His grace alone that sustained me, but I never dealt with the roots of my passionate commitment to perfection, and they cast long shadows. I was afraid to be less than "the best."

I felt like ever since I had accepted Christ into my life, I made good choices for the wrong reasons. Sure, I never slept around, smoked, or drank, what I considered the "big" sins. I am glad that I did not rebel and walk away from God; I am happy that I threw myself into serving Him. But I *am* sorry it took me so long to truly understand that "perfect love drives out fear" (1 John 4:18). I tried so hard to be perfect because I was afraid if I wasn't, God would turn on me as my father had. I didn't want God to see in me whatever it was my father saw, what had made him so angry, what had made him hate me.

So I committed to be the best, perfect Christian woman, even if it killed me. And it nearly did.

The stakes got much higher as I became more recognizable. I enjoyed being president of the Junior Christian Endeavor at church, and it was fun to sing the lead role in the school musical, but as the years went on I invested more and more of myself into how I was received and perceived by the public. That became the plumb line to me; it measured the value of my life.

My first taste of "fame" was at a Christian holiday camp in England. I was twenty-four years old and employed by British Youth for Christ as a musical evangelist. My role was to support other musicians and help lead worship, but for this camp I was asked to prepare a solo concert with the band. Graham Kendrick and a few other friends wrote songs for me. I thought it was going to be fun until the night approached. I suddenly realized that if the concert was a disaster, I stood alone.

I was petrified. The day came, and the auditorium was packed. I had recorded two of my songs on a "single," and the record company was there that night for the debut. Before I went on, I sat backstage with my head between my knees. I felt as if I would either vomit or pass out, but there was no time for either. I heard them announce my name.

The concert went incredibly well. I left the stage relieved and thinking that now I would go out with my friends for a burger just as we always had before. But no. I was whisked off to the record table to sign records. They sold out that evening, and everyone was exuberant. I had wanted my life to be used by God, and this seemed to be the breakthrough I had been looking for.

I had never experienced that kind of manic attention before. Everything changed for me that night. Christian magazines wanted to do interviews. Radio stations wanted my opinion on everything. I soon received invitations to sing all over the country.

Even though that first concert went very well, it did not help my anxiety the next time or the time after that. I was very nervous, so I began to concentrate on the exterior of my life. If I had to meet with a record company representative or an interviewer, I bought a new outfit. I did not make a lot of money with YFC, so I opened store credit cards. I couldn't bear to face new people unless I had carefully wrapped up the outside of my life. As my life moved on and new opportunities were given me, my successes convinced me that I was okay.

It was amazing to me to watch people respond to the Lord working through me. When I would feel lost and alone, as if I did not belong anywhere, I was comforted by those who seemed to be helped. It gave me a sense of purpose, of definition, to know God was with me.

When it became apparent to me in the hospital that my public ministry was coming to an end, and I could no longer keep going, my life felt empty and hopeless. When it became obvious I was letting people down and that some people seemed happy to see me falter, I felt terror.

Turning Point

"So what is the worst thing that could happen to you, Sheila?" the doctor asked.

"I am afraid I will be swept away, forgotten, alone. I know there are a couple of people who would gladly destroy my life."

"Sheila, who is your trust in?" he asked me. "Do you feel as if the Lord has left you?"

That question was a turning point in my journey because my answer was a resounding no! I had written a poem in my journal the previous evening:

> *I never knew You lived so close to the floor,*
> *but every time I am bowed down,*
> *crushed by this weight of grief,*
> *I feel Your hand on my head,*
> *Your breath on my cheek,*
> *Your tears on my neck.*
> *You never tell me to pull myself together,*
> *to stem the flow of many years.*
> *You simply stay by my side*
> *for as long as it takes,*
> *so close to the floor.*

Until this crisis I had never known what an awesome companion the Lord longs to be. I had spent so many years trying to make Him proud of me, determined to never fail, that I missed the most amazing gift of all: to be able, as I once heard a young poet say from stage, "to bury my face in the mane of the Lion of Judah."

I read *The Lion, the Witch and the Wardrobe* by C. S. Lewis again recently. There is so much to learn from children's stories. The part that is most memorable to me happens when the children are preparing to meet Aslan the lion for the very first time. They are afraid to come face-to-face with such a powerful animal, and their guides acknowledge the appropriateness of that reaction.

"Aslan is a lion—the Lion, the great Lion."

"Ooh!" said Susan, "I'd thought he was a man. Is he—quite safe? I shall feel rather nervous about meeting a lion."

"Safe?" said Mr Beaver . . . "Who said anything about safe? 'Course he isn't safe. But he's good. He's the King, I tell you."[1]

Running to hide our faces in God is not like seeking the comfort and familiarity of a childhood blanket that allows us to tune out the realities of our lives. God is a mighty lion, whose roar is heard in every corner of the world. Still, when you are in trouble, you can hide your face from Him or run to Him and let Him hide you in His mane. There you will find the strength and freedom to live your life.

Age-Old Fears

In the Bible, fear is first mentioned in Genesis 3:10, when Adam said to the Lord, "I heard you in the garden, and I was afraid." Fear entered our world at the fall. Adam was afraid because he knew he had disobeyed God. The peace and tranquility of the garden of Eden was lost forever. Once humankind had listened to the serpent, good and evil became players on our stage. From that point in human history, fear either threw us on our faces before God or caused us to hide our faces from Him.

David was very familiar with fear. In Psalm 56:3, he wrote,

"When I am afraid, I put my trust in you," and he cried out in Psalm 69:1, "Save me, O God, for the waters have come up to my neck." He also wrote these magnificent, life-sustaining words:

> *The Lord is my light and my salvation—*
>   *whom shall I fear?*
> *The Lord is the stronghold of my life—*
>   *of whom shall I be afraid?*
>   (Psalm 27:1)

To David, fear was a reaction to forces that were coming against him; it was not a response, not a way of life. As an older man, he was able to deal with fear and the threats of his enemies because of how he lived as a young man. David had been a shepherd boy, whose job was to make sure no harm came to the sheep. From time to time, lions or bears would try to carry a lamb away, but David was right there, slingshot in hand, ready to fight for the lamb's life. In the quiet, early years of his life, hidden away in a field, he made the choices to become the man he would later be. If David had run away as a boy, he would have run away as an adult; instead, he grabbed hold of his fear and reined it in.

Facing My Fears

Now it was my turn to face and rein in my fear. Courage is developed by embracing our greatest fears and not being deterred by them. I used to wait for courage, as if it were a gift that would be dropped by heaven into my heart, instantly transforming me into the kind of woman I imagined I could be.

But I had to start with the kind of woman that I was and, by pressing on, find courage. My favorite character in *The Wizard of Oz* is the Cowardly Lion. Underneath the false bravado, the

Cowardly Lion is a very scared creature that believes if he can just make it to the Emerald City, he will be home free. His expressed intention for the journey is to ask the wizard for the gift of courage. As he sets off on the journey with Dorothy, the Tin Man, the Scarecrow, and Toto, he encounters all sorts of hazards. But because the travelers are committed to one another, they risk going beyond their comfort level. The Cowardly Lion does not allow his fear to disable him. By the time they discover that the wizard is just a man, the Lion is no longer afraid.

Eleanor Roosevelt said:

> You gain strength, courage and confidence by every experience in which you really stop to look fear in the face. You are able to say to yourself, "I lived through this horror; I can take the next thing that comes along. . . ." You must do the thing you think you cannot do.[2]

That is how things began to change for me. I knew that in seeking my security and strength in the approval of others, I would rise or fall at their dictate. Fear of anger was making it easy for me to be controlled by angry people, but I must be controlled only by Christ.

After a couple of weeks of therapy, I decided to start listening to what God had to say about my life. It was not easy, but I knew that it would give me courage to be real with other people, to be vulnerable. The Lord's love is a strong love that does not flatter or overlook our sinful nature: "For he knows how we are formed, he remembers that we are dust" (Psalm 103:14).

In the hospital, I began to pray the Psalms out loud. David was passionately honest in his relationship with God. He didn't close down as I had learned to do. I discovered what liberty lies in voicing my fears. I wrote:

Why do I shutter my heart?
Why do I keep it closed
on days when it seems about to break?
Why can't I let it go?
Why can't I ask for help
and admit that I'm barely alive?
I think if I voice it
I'd have to believe it
to hear all the sadness.
I just could not bear it.
That's why I shutter my heart.

While I used to be afraid to name my fear, as if voicing fears would make them more real and give them more power, I now discovered the opposite was true. I could scream aloud to the Lord and still be standing. I wasn't evaporated by my own words.

Fear of man will prove to be a snare,
but whoever trusts in the LORD is kept safe.

(PROVERBS 29:25)

Fear still creeps up on me at times, like when I step onstage in front of a large crowd or wait for the results of a biopsy of a tumor that looked suspicious or find myself challenged to do something I've never done before. When I hear fear's familiar drumbeat pounding in my heart, I find that talking about my feelings to the Lord and to those who love me takes away its power to rule over me. I cry sometimes if that helps, but I remind myself whose I am. Fear still affects me—as it did King David—but it does not control me.

I sought the LORD, and he answered me;
he delivered me from all my fears.

(PSALM 34:4)

Fear of Intimacy

As I grew older, my childhood fear had grown into a general uneasiness and a mistrust of people. Fear and intimacy do not make good traveling companions, so I lived a very busy, crowded, solitary life.

I had felt so alone for so long. Now I began to understand that the greatest barrier to intimacy is fear—fear of being known, fear of being rejected, fear of facing the truth about ourselves. John Donne, the sixteenth-century poet, wrote these familiar but profound words:

> No man is an island, entire of itself; every man is a piece of the continent, a part of the main. . . . Any man's death diminishes me because I am involved in mankind, and therefore never send to know for whom the bell tolls; it tolls for thee.

What Donne showed in that masterly quote is a deep spiritual truth: we are involved in one another's lives. Yet he hints at a human problem: at times a fear of connection drives us away from one another. We are afraid to be known because we might be rejected. We are afraid to be known because at some deep level we fear that the truth about us, when out in the open and reflected back to us through someone else's eyes, will be shocking to *ourselves.*

That had to be a very present reality for the Samaritan woman at the well who made her way to get water when she would never have to face condemning eyes. So we struggle with this human dichotomy: we long to be known because we are lonely, and we fear being known because we may then be loneliest of all.

Fear of Disapproval or Failure

Part of coming to terms with fear has been accepting that there is good and bad in me and good and bad in others. Jesus' statement,

"Love your enemies" (Matthew 5:44), presupposes that enemies exist. We do have enemies, people who would rather see us fail than succeed. We know, too, from the story of Job that at times God will allow our lives to be disrupted. The lesson for me is that God is passionately committed to the kind of woman I will *become*, not to what I *do*.

This simple truth has revolutionized my life. It is the opposite of what we hear on television or read online, and is contrary to what we at times in the church seem to believe as well. We place so much emphasis on success and achievement, on accomplishment and numbers. But God is singularly unimpressed with all the paraphernalia we have attached to our faith.

I am learning that what God cares about is who I am when the lights are off and the crowds have gone home. This truth also means that whatever comes into my life, whether it is what I would choose or not, can be used by the Lord to mold my life if I will trust Him.

I used to live in fear, wondering what might happen to me, what someone might say about me. But now, as Thomas à Kempis said, I am learning to "receive from Thy hand good and evil, sweet and bitter, joy and sorrow, and to give Thee thanks for all that happeneth to me."[3]

I recently relearned this lesson when a neighbor asked to hold a Bible study in my house on a night that I had already committed to play basketball with my son. She made it clear she was disappointed and that she thought I made the wrong choice, but that didn't matter to me. Keeping my word to my son honored Christ more than impressing my neighbor.

One of the greatest gifts God gives us is peace of mind. Perhaps, like me, you feel you can only find peace on a desert island. The demands of our lives constantly pester us, like flies on a hot summer day. But even though life is difficult and demanding, it remains true that the perfect love of Jesus has the power to drive out our most devastating fears.

Fear and Anger

Through ongoing counseling and personal reflection, I looked at how my fear had manifested itself over the years and realized that even though I was afraid of anger in others, I responded to that fear with, yes, anger. Silent anger. I used it as protection, a shield to hide behind.

One writer has compared repressed anger to having a basement full of pent-up, angry dogs. I like that illustration, for that is just how it felt to me. What made it worse was that I must have somehow snuck in the dogs when no one was looking. After all, I am a Christian woman, and women are not supposed to be angry.

More often than not, if a man is angry he is viewed as a man of passion, of principle, but an angry woman is quite another matter. It is too easy to dismiss her as neurotic or strident, and if she happens to be single, well, she may as well be quiet and break out the knitting!

Anger born out of pain needs to find a place of release, but how do women do that? Many of us struggle with anger that has little to do with righteousness. I don't think that I have ever heard a sermon on how to handle anger, even though I believe we have churches full of angry people.

As I sat in a group meeting at the hospital one morning, talking about some of the most painful experiences of my life, someone said, "You sound very detached, Sheila. Some of this stuff is pretty recent. Why aren't you angry?"

I was shocked and disturbed by what this other patient was saying.

He continued, "You sound like you are telling someone else's story. Don't you care about your life?"

I did not say much more that morning, but for the rest of the day, it was as if I were running old black-and-white movies of my life through my head.

My first taste of anger—from my father to me as a child—had affected my whole life. I would do anything I could to diffuse an angry situation. Angry words or tone of voice—spoken even by myself—seemed to me to signal that something drastic was about to happen. I never gave myself permission to be angry; when things happened in my life that I should have been angry about, I just stuffed the feelings down. I packed the cellar as tightly as I could, ground my teeth and clenched my fists, and said nothing.

Occasionally, when I wasn't being vigilant, little bits would escape, leaking out in sudden outbursts or sarcasm, but I seldom threw those dogs any meat at all. The hungrier they got, the more they fought to escape, the more I guarded them. I talked louder or worked harder until they tired of their barking and quieted down for a while.

Facing My Anger

It is very difficult to begin to deal with anger issues when you are thirty-four and have lived with them since you were five. Following my therapist's advice, I wrote down everything I could think of that I was angry about. But I didn't know what to do with it. I stared at the seemingly random events scribbled before me, unsure of what came next. So I began to pray. I felt as if the Lord was the only one who could deal with the sadness, the rage, the loneliness, the fear, and the waves of emotion that were sweeping over me and not be diminished by them.

Once again, the Psalms modeled raw emotion for me. One

from the days of Israel's captivity in Babylon contains some of the strongest language in the Bible:

> *Daughter Babylon, doomed to destruction,*
> *happy is the one who repays you*
> *according to what you have done to us . . .*
> *The one who seizes your infants*
> *and dashes them against the rocks.*
>
> (PSALM 137:8–9)

Strong words from God's people. Several editions of prayer books or worship books have edited these words out. Eugene Peterson, in his book *Answering God*, says that these "Psalmectomies" are wrong, reasoning: "They are wrong-headed because our hate needs to be prayed, not suppressed."[4]

What a liberating concept: that our hate—our anger—needs to be prayed. Burying it will not make it go away. Suppressing it contaminates our souls. If we fail to take it to God, it will leak out and destroy the world—not to mention us.

As I began to look at my own life, to listen to the things that made me angry and give them a voice, I realized that *my anger always sprang out of fear.* When I felt I was being threatened in some way, I became angry inside in order to defend myself—the dogs of rage would rise up to my defense. But I was never comfortable voicing my anger. As I mentioned before, it would either slip out in sarcastic comments or I would withdraw from the situation before the anger escaped. It was as if my trust was in the sheepdog, not the Shepherd. The sheepdog looked ready to devour anything that invaded his land, so I stuck close to him. Anger offered me a way of gaining control when I felt out of control.

I am learning now to trust the Shepherd to be my defender. For me it is a daily, sometimes hourly, relinquishing of control of my life and my destiny to God. When I feel myself getting angry now, I take a step back. I go into another room by myself, sit at the Shepherd's feet, and I tell Him what I am feeling. When I forget to do that, or choose not to do that, I ask for forgiveness. I do not take this lightly. It is no fun to be the recipient of my anger. Scripture, in fact, tells us to avoid such people (Proverbs 22:24). Through the years, the anger has subsided as I have consciously brought all the broken pieces of my life to Christ. It is one thing to feel as if power has been taken from you as a defenseless child. It is quite another to gladly surrender it as an adult to a risen Savior!

For any number of reasons, many of us live on the edge of a volcano, shaken by ominous rumbles that threaten our footing. So I say with Eugene Peterson, let's pray our anger out; let's cry out our hurt and pain and fear until we have no tears left. Anger needs to be expressed, and it is much better for us to cry it out to God than to machine-gun our friends with it.

One of the most wonderful aspects of our relationship with Christ is that we don't have to talk—He understands. When you are in pain, it is so exhausting to have to try and explain to others what you are feeling. What a relief it is to be able to lie down in a field with the Shepherd and not have to say a word.

There is a mystery at play here: the broken bread principle. Remember the story in John 6? A little boy brings his lunch to Jesus, who blesses it, breaks it, and passes it out to His friends to distribute to the crowd. A miracle occurs. One boy's lunch multiplies and feeds five thousand people. There is enough for everyone.

We can allow fear and anger to cripple our souls, or we can bring our devastating circumstances to Christ and ask Him to bless us in our brokenness and to feed His body, the church. Shortly after hymn writer George Matheson became engaged to be married, he lost his eyesight. His fiancée left him. Facing loss and an unknown future, he could have become a bitter, angry man. I would imagine that he tasted both bitterness and anger, but he did not feast on them or let them feast on him. He took his burden to Christ, and you and I are fed by his words:

> *O Love that will not let me go,*
> *I rest my weary soul in thee;*
> *I give thee back the life I owe,*
> *That in thine ocean depths its flow*
> *May richer, fuller be.*
> *O Joy that seekest me through pain,*
> *I cannot close my heart to thee;*
> *I trace the rainbow through the rain,*
> *And feel the promise is not vain*
> *That morn shall tearless be.*

We are people who need each other. We need each other to be honest, to struggle with the pain of life, to look for traces of redemption in the darkest moments. And if the whole purpose of our lives on this earth is to glorify God and enjoy Him forever, then I believe He is the one to whom we can bring the emotions that tear at our hearts. As we bare our souls before Him, He will trade our unbearable burdens for a load that we can carry.

> *Father God, hear our prayers.*
> *We bring our fear to You.*
> *We bring our rage to You.*
> *We bring the broken pieces of our lives.*
> *Teach us to live lightly,*
> *casting our cares on You.*
> *Thank You that we can bury our faces in You.*
> *Amen.*

Fear and shame have clothed me
like a suit of cheap perfume—
impossible to point to,
but felt in every room.

Chapter 6

Paralyzed by Shame

I lugged around inside me a dead
weight of not-good-enoughness.

—Lewis Smedes, *Shame and Grace*

It was always spring in the garden. Every morning the sweet perfume of a hundred different flowers melted together to create the fragrance of the day. The sun was warm and gentle. Each new day was filled with endless possibilities; good things rested under every leaf. Animals leaned on one another as they napped at peace in the shade of a tree. This was a paradise.

A golden cord ran through the hearts of Adam and Eve that also touched the trees, the flowers, the animals. Nothing was untouched by the cord that led back to the Lord of the garden. Adam and Eve were asleep when the serpent approached them. He began to sing a different song, a strange song, discordant with the melody of the garden. It woke them up. "There is more," he whispered to them, "so much more."

Eve looked at the strange creature. It was hard to see him clearly because the sun was in her eyes.

"There is more. There is much more. He is keeping things from you. You are not all you could be."

What could he possibly mean, more?

"You know so little, child," the serpent said pityingly. "It's there for the taking."

Eve looked at the serpent; she looked at the tree. God had told them to stay away. Now she wondered why. If this truly was their garden, surely they could do what they wanted. Eve stretched her hand toward the fruit. Not an animal moved. She took it and bit into it—a sweet, strong taste.

She gave some to Adam. "Taste this. This is better than all the rest."

Adam raised the fruit to his lips and let the juice run down his face. Just then, the sun vanished behind a cloud and the animals ran for cover. Some of the smaller creatures were crushed in the scuffle, but no one even noticed. Eve felt a chill in the air. She and Adam looked at each other, and they knew that something was wrong, very wrong. So little had happened, but everything was different. The moment they decided to taste the part of life they were missing, everything changed. Their eyes were "opened," and what they saw horrified them.

They turned away from each other and quickly assembled garments made of fig leaves to cover themselves. But it wasn't enough; they still felt naked. All day they hid under the cover of a tree, but in the evening they heard God's voice. He was asking for them, asking why they were hiding.

Adam and Eve tried to hide under layers of clothing. We have been adding to those layers ever since, not in clothing, but in layer upon layer of internal veiling. Even Adam and Eve felt the new, unfamiliar feeling that sat, heavy as a stone, inside both of them. They did not know its name, but we do: it is called shame.

Until that cataclysmic moment, they had trusted each other. Then, suddenly, sin caused them to hide from God and from each other. I believe that the seeds of all our relational ills can be seen in this Genesis story. Sin brought us into a world of fear, a fear closely linked to shame.

I have read several books on shame, which seems to be defined in a variety of ways. Most people distinguish between guilt and shame, defining guilt as the feeling that accompanies having *done* something wrong, and shame as the feeling that you *are* something wrong.

Shame's Deep Roots

Where would I start to explain to you a feeling that is as familiar to me as my face in the mirror? For as long as I can remember, I have felt the breath of the racehorse Shame on my neck. We are old traveling companions. I can be as impatient as anyone else with the "I tripped over my dog when I was two, and I will never be able to trust again" rhetoric of pop psychology. I do know, however, that the significant events of early life have the power to shape our futures.

Look through my window for a moment, and you will see a very happy family: a loving mother and father, three children, and a little brown dachshund named Heidi. Suddenly, overnight, everything changes. A blood clot wipes out a part of the father's brain and the picture of "normal" is gone. Life moves from safe to scary overnight. And then, suddenly, without an explanation, he's gone.

I—the younger daughter—fell from being invincible to having to protect myself at all costs. *Don't let anyone see inside,* I would tell myself. *Perhaps someone will see whatever it was that your daddy saw. Perhaps that person will leave—and you know how much that hurts.*

In the hospital, with my mom at my side, I relived these

childhood events. So often we perceive pain as a negative force to be avoided at all costs. But just as the pain of childbirth brings new life into the world, so the pain of walking through the darkest valleys brings the traveler to the land that lies beyond. As Mum and I talked through the times I had tried to erase from my mind, I was able to bring adult perspective to childhood pain. Just to hear from someone I love and trust that what had happened with my dad was not my fault, that he loved me very much and would have been proud of me, was like drops of fresh water to a parched soul.

Not Up to Standard

As I allowed this fresh perspective to take center stage for a while, I saw how for so long I had been chasing the image of perfection, just like a perfect china cup. Let me explain. When I was a student in London, I bought a china cup from the Reject China Shop. It was only a few doors away from Harrods, the magnificent department store, and it stocked the items that did not quite meet Harrods's standard. Sometimes if you looked hard enough, you could find a piece that seemed perfect. I was sure I had found such a piece; it must have slipped through quality control. I held it up to the light and couldn't see a single flaw.

With some pride in my find, I took it home and put on the kettle to make some tea and christen my cup. But as soon as I poured the boiling liquid into the cup, the china cracked from top to bottom. The heat of the water exposed the flaw that was imperceptible to the human eye.

That was how I felt about my life. On the outside, everything looked great. But if it ever got too hot, I was sure I would crack from top to bottom. I had felt this way for as long as I could remember. The more unsure I felt about myself, the more I picked up on people's reactions to me. I took things personally that I should have been able to slough off.

I remember the first show I did years ago as the host for the new BBC show representing the best of contemporary Christian and traditional black gospel music. Makeup artists and wardrobe people fussed over me endlessly. We taped the show, and it aired a few nights later. I watched it later with a bunch of friends. I thought I looked pretty good, until a friend's six-year-old son said, "Wow, you look a lot fatter on television!"

Everyone laughed, and I did, too, but I was dying of embarrassment inside.

A few weeks later I was on the studio floor with the band rehearsing, and suddenly over the whole audio system I heard the director yell, "Makeup! Do something with her ears." The makeup girl ran out and fussed a bit with my hair and then yelled into my microphone, "I'm a makeup artist, not a miracle worker!"

For the rest of the day, every time I turned around, someone was looking at my ears. I could have sold tickets. Afterward I asked the girl what was wrong with my ears.

"They stick out, dear."

Someone else added, "We better make sure that there are no strong winds in the studio!"

Everyone went off laughing, and I went to my dressing room and wept.

The next day I looked in the yellow pages for plastic surgeons. I found one clinic close to where I was living. I called and asked how much it would be to have my ears pinned back. She gave me two prices, one for a general anesthetic and one for a local. Because I already felt guilty about spending money on something like that, I went for the local. I was petrified. I hate the sight of blood, particularly mine, but my mind was set. As they wheeled me into the operating room, I prayed that God would not let them mess up and cut my ears off!

The surgery was horrible. They gave me four injections in each ear and then began to cut. I passed out on the spot, so the general anesthetic would have been a waste of money! I left the hospital with a numb face and my head wrapped in bandages, but convinced that I would now feel better about myself.

I did not. My ears were no longer the focal point of the show, but when deep distress is internal, you cannot heal that with surgery. If the trouble is inside, you take it with you wherever you go.

Deep down I believed that my imperfections, whether physical or internal, had made my father turn from me. If I could just seem flawless to myself, to God, and to others—like a perfect Harrods china cup—I would be loved. The truth I was beginning to realize in the hospital is that Christ is the only perfect cup.

The Shame Profile

While in the hospital, I had the opportunity to attend a talk on the subject of shame. As the psychologist outlined the "shame profile," many of us shifted uncomfortably in our chairs. This is what it looks like:

1. *Shame includes an enduring negative self-image.* No matter how many wonderful things are happening in your life, none of it means anything to you because of how you feel about yourself inside.
2. *Shame is highly "performance conscious."* You always feel you are "on." You are so anxious to please and to be needed that you measure your worth by what you can produce, as if that will give you value in the eyes of yourself and others.
3. *Shame makes you unaware of personal boundaries.* You're not sure who you are as separate from someone else; you're not sure where you "end" and others "begin." You find it virtually impossible to stand up for yourself

and say no. It's easier to allow others to make decisions and choose for you. You reveal inappropriate personal details of your life to people you have only recently met in an attempt to feel connected to someone.

4. *Shame festers in people who are "wounded."* Underneath the surface of your life, there is a wound that has never healed. You nurse it and maintain it. It gives you identity.

5. *Shame is accompanied by a pervading tiredness.* There is no place for joy in shame. This means you are always tired and weighed down by life. Burdens overwhelm you.

6. *Shame has a built-in radar system, tuned to keeping every-one happy and at peace.* A sense of shame makes you overly responsible. You make it your job to ensure every-thing is running smoothly and everyone else is happy.

7. *Shame makes you ignore your own needs like a martyr.* Because shame tells you that you are no good, you seek to balance the scales by ignoring your own legitimate needs. Attempts to please and appease others are always more important than listening to and caring for yourself.

8. *Shame tends toward addictive behavior, which can mani-fest itself in over-involvement in work or ministry.* You are so ashamed of yourself that you work harder and longer in a desperate search for that elusive peace. (This is a huge issue in the church.)

9. *Shame has no concept of "normal."* If you have grown up with unhealthy behavior in your family, you perceive that to be the norm. You lack the perspective to know what "normal" should look like. For example, if you grew up with someone yelling in your face, that became familiar to you; you don't realize it is unhealthy behav-ior you do not have to live with.

10. *Shame makes it difficult to trust others.* You tend to be

very guarded around others, wondering what their agenda is for your life. It is hard to let anyone in, because you're sure that person will not like what she sees. This behavior can border on paranoia.

11. *Shame makes you possessive in relationships.* Out of a feeling of unworthiness and fear of abandonment, you cling to the people in your life, afraid that if they leave, no one will be there to take their place.

12. *Shame has a high need for control.* Life is scary to a shame-based person; the only bearable way to survive is to maintain control.

It is easy to see why wounded people adopt some of these patterns. If the one who should protect you from pain (such as a parent or spouse) becomes the perpetrator of the pain, it is easiest to throw up walls, so you won't be hurt again in the future; trust becomes a major issue.

I recognized myself in many of the points discussed that evening. I had never heard of personal boundaries (we don't have those in Scotland!), but as I listened to what was being said, it began to make sense to me. For example, I have had a very difficult time developing intimate friendships. I kept my true self pretty guarded and safe. But if you talked to viewers of *The 700 Club*, they would probably disagree, saying that I was a very open person whom they knew well. The strange thing is, it felt safe to unburden my soul to a large, anonymous crowd, much safer than to a few people who really knew me.

Shame, Guilt, and Shamelessness

Shame is so dehumanizing. There is no dignity or strength in shame. It tells us that we are worthless and hopeless. Shame is much more damaging than good old-fashioned guilt because it seems so hopeless. If we have *done* something wrong, we can make an active attempt to rectify the situation. But if we *are* something wrong, what hope is there?

As I uncovered the shame that had drawn me in like quicksand, I also realized that, though it was important that I understand my past, I could not *blame* my past. Shifting the blame will never make anything better. It is only as I step up to the plate and accept full responsibility for my life that I will ever find peace and healing.

Again, I note that there is a great difference between the unhealthy shame that makes us crawl away into a corner and the kind of healthy shame called conviction that shows us when we are wrong and need to change our ways. The Bible calls us to live with integrity and humility, constantly confessing our sins to one another and loving one another. But it's important to remember that this biblical call to face our sins and our human frailties is neither the shame that makes us feel as if we must run and hide our brokenness, nor a shamelessness that tries to release us from any accountability to anyone or anything.

I saw a story on CNN that was capturing the aftermath of a murder trial in Philadelphia. The reporter was interviewing the mother of the young victim. She had such a ravaged look on her face. The reporter asked her if she was glad that it was all over and that the accused had been convicted. She didn't say anything for a moment; then she said, "Do you know what that boy said to me? He said, 'So what if I killed your son?' My baby is gone, and that is all he had to say."

Tears rolled down my cheeks as I saw the look of utter disbelief in the eyes of this bereaved mother, numbed by the indifference of a cold-blooded killer.

Surely in a world that so often has lost the map and compass to living with integrity and compassion, the only hope is the church, but I wonder if we, as the church, are looking in the right direction.

It Is Not Our Job to Shame the World

Jesus never shamed anyone. He did, however, call out some of the church leaders on their hypocrisy. He was angry when they turned a sanctuary into a marketplace. But He never shamed people.

Remember the scene where a crowd of religious men threw a woman at Jesus' feet, demanding their pound of flesh. She had been caught in adultery and by law should have been stoned to death. Jesus said to them, "All right, if that is how you want to handle this, then let's spray everyone with the same dye. If you have never sinned, please feel free to throw the first stone."

Slowly the crowd slipped away and left the woman lying in the dust.

Jesus picked her up and said to her, "They have all gone home. No one is left to accuse you, and neither do I—but don't do this anymore; you are worth more than this." (I have paraphrased this story from John 8.)

Jesus' compassion was a running theme. He also treated Mary Magdalene, a woman who had been delivered from seven demons, with respect and dignity. And when He was being tortured to death, Jesus still made time for the thief dying beside Him.

Christ recognized what we have forgotten: that every single human being on this planet has been created in the *imago dei*, the image of God. It is easy for us as the church to tear apart talk show hosts and their nutty guests, to judge women who make their way into abortion clinics, to stand self-righteously above gay rights activists, but every human being *must* be treated with dignity and respect, because the mark of the image of God rests upon us all, no matter whether we acknowledge that or not.

I sense that sometimes we in the church devote too much time trying to keep the mud of the world off "our" shoes and too little time washing it off "theirs." As long as we simply point fingers, why should anyone listen to us? It is not our job to try and shame the world, but to love them with the love of Christ. After Jesus looked at a man or a woman, he or she was never the same again. (Remember the Samaritan woman at the well?)

It saddens me that many times Christians' voices are heard publicly only when we are against something. Yes, we are living in a very sick and depraved world, and those things need to be addressed. But will we draw people to us and to Christ if we stand and tell the world they have brought their pain upon themselves and walk away without helping them?

Christ spoke the truth in all its heartbreaking power to everyone He encountered. Jesus even left the crowd to have dinner with a tax collector who had been ripping people off for years. We don't know what was said, but we do know that after this encounter with Jesus, the tax collector was a changed man. His heart was so transformed that he not only repaid what he had stolen from others, he paid back four times what he had taken and then gave half of his wealth to the poor (Luke 19:1–10). Jesus took the fierce and piercing light of who He is to every situation, but He went in love.

When a Christian Falters

We come to Christ to be forgiven for our sins, to be given a new heart, and then we are asked to care for one another, to be the church. But too often the church doesn't know how to be the church. In his book *Guilt and Grace*, Paul Tournier wrote:

> The church proclaims the grace of God. And moralism, which is the negation of it, always creeps [back] into its bosom. . . .

> Grace becomes conditional. Judgment appears. . . . I see its
> ravages every day in . . . all the Christian churches.[1]

By our behavior, Christians say to one another that as long
as we are all performing "normally" (whatever that means) we
will walk together. But if one of us stumbles—gets caught in a
lie, falls off the sobriety wagon, has an affair—then the rest of us
will simply keep walking, praying that we will learn to be better
judges of character next time. We allow our disappointment to
become distance, confirming the worst fears of the person who
is left lying in the dust: "I am a bad person; why did I even hope
that God could love me?"

The words of St. Paul have been very helpful to me. Even
though he was being used in unprecedented ways to build up
the fledgling church, Paul still struggled with his sinful nature.
"For I do not do the good I want to do, but the evil I do not
want to do—this I keep on doing" (Romans 7:19). Paul made
it very clear that we are in a battle with our nature and that, at
times, our sinful nature will win out. But he never used that as
an excuse; he continued to press on to be more like Christ.

I cry for mercy for those in the dust, and yet I understand
the fears of those who wonder what we, as Christians, are supposed to do about the sin and brokenness among us.

Too often we Christians see only two possibilities for dealing
with human frailty: (1) we distance ourselves from those who
are in trouble, in the earnest desire that this will wake them up
and they will straighten themselves out; (2) we ignore the warn-
ings we note in others' lives in a desire to respect their privacy.

I suggest a third way: that we speak the truth to one another,
that we care enough to reach out, and that, no matter what we
find, we do not let go.

Like a mother sending her daughter off to college for the first time, Paul is very careful to instruct the church in how to deal with problems that will inevitably occur: "Brothers and sisters, if someone is caught in a sin, you who live by the Spirit should restore that person gently. But watch yourselves, or you also may be tempted. Carry each other's burdens, and in this way you will fulfill the law of Christ" (Galatians 6:1–2).

It was interesting to me to note that the Greek word we translate as *restore* is the same word that would be used in a hospital setting if someone were brought in with a broken limb; it denotes brokenness and the need for time and care.

It is also interesting that Paul's words do not come across as a suggestion, but as a command. At times we are reluctant to get involved when someone is in trouble because we do not know what to say. While I can certainly relate to that, it is not scriptural. Other times we do not reach out because the person's trouble is too much like our own, and his or her struggle is rocking our boat. And sometimes we simply have no mercy, or it would demand too much of us to try and get involved.

As I write this book, I have watched some Christian public figures deal with crises lived out in a public spotlight. How have we, as the church, struggled to come to terms with what was revealed about these people? How should we deal with these crises? I have noticed a variety of responses to these people in trouble:

1. We must save their careers at all cost.
2. We should fix their problems quickly and quietly, behind the scenes.
3. Let's decide who is going to be the winner and who is going to be the loser, and back the winner.
4. The quick fixes are not working, so let's walk away.
5. We should say we saw it coming.
6. Let's move on with our lives and leave them in the dust.

I saw a television special on Mike Tyson the other evening. (Google tells me this man is number four on the list of the top ten violent celebrities!) It made me think that we in the Christian community do not deal with one another very differently than the world deals with its heroes. It was very clear to those around Mike Tyson that he was a man filled with rage, but that very rage made him a killer boxer, so instead of caring for him, the people around him marketed and sold his flaw.

Many Christians are no different. We see what is happening behind the scenes with a person in public life, but that person is so effective and successful at what he or she does, or is so powerful, that we turn a blind eye. We reason away our concern by telling ourselves, "God is using that person." Well, God spoke through Balaam's donkey, so I don't find that argument very convincing!

The problem I have with that is it shows no love whatsoever toward the person in trouble. We walk with him or her for as long as we can until the situation blows up, and then we move on, leaving one more broken, used-up life in our wake.

Many of the same people from the network who had distanced themselves from me years before later apologized. They explained they simply didn't know what to say. I have come to believe that the experience taught us all something—after all, how else will we grow? Failure can be an awesome teacher if we invite Christ into the process.

It was good for me that my friends distanced themselves, because it ultimately forced me to face my terrible fear of rejection and bring it to Jesus. It was good for them, too, because it caused them to examine how we react to a life in crisis. (In falling short, we can ask the Lord to teach us how to respond, so that the next time someone is in pain, we will be better equipped to deal with it.)

But at the time of my depression, the silence I encountered from those closest to me added to my feelings of utter hopelessness.

I had failed; therefore, I was a failure. The hopelessness I felt was so pervasive that I ignored the calls of one old friend who wanted to come see me. I felt so ashamed that I could not look at anyone.

Shame and Grace

Too many of us are at war within ourselves. When that is the case, the following questions arise: How can you extend grace to others when you have not received it yourself? Where do you go when you feel flawed? Where do you find healing when you know you are sick?

For me, the only place to go was to the feet of the only One who is perfect, the only One who fully understands how flawed I am and yet who loves me completely.

Jesus said, "Come to me, all you who are weary and burdened, and I will give you rest" (Matthew 11:28). When our Lord was brutally executed, He took upon Himself all the filth and decay of a diseased world. He knew that we could not make it on our own, so He took our place. Wherever He encountered darkness, He brought light. When He met people who were in hiding, He called them out. Whether it was a "scarlet woman" or a little man hiding up a tree, His words were words of healing and hope and freedom. Isaiah told us, "The people walking in darkness have seen a great light; on those living in the land of deep darkness a light has dawned" (Isaiah 9:2).

I have a friend who is a missionary on the border between Thailand and Cambodia. He has a heart for people suffering from leprosy in the refugee camps. He and his colleagues began to spend time with those men and women, doing what they could to aid them physically and spiritually. Eventually a church was born, right there in the middle of a leper camp. During one of their services, a man who had been among the first to make a commitment to following Christ said, "One of the most wonderful things that has happened to me since I met Jesus is that now I can look you in the face. I was too ashamed before because of my disfigurement, but if Jesus loves me so much, then I think that I can hold my head up high."

That is how it is supposed to be for us all. Jesus has restored our dignity. What we sold so cheaply in Eden, He has bought back for us at a great price. We all struggle with our humanity, with our soulishness, but cleansing is not found in the shadows; it is found in the burning light.

The word *grace* is now as familiar to me as wind or rain, although it took me some time to be able to receive this lavish gift. Grace was never meant to be rationed, something we nibble on to get us through tough times. It is meant to soak us to (and through) the skin and fill us so full that we can hardly catch our breath. My problem was that I had such a tight grasp on my life, there was very little room into which grace could be poured.

I remember running to the altar at the church I visited while in the hospital, dragging my shame and grief behind me. Everything was different from that day on. Grace gave me the courage to face my biggest fears and the harshest truths about my life because it held on to me and never let go. I felt an overwhelming thankfulness deep in my bones. I knew I could never pay for this awesome gift, but it had my name on it, and it would never be taken away.

True grace is so overwhelming you are compelled to extend it to those around you, whether they deserve it or not. George MacDonald said:

Whether he pay you what you count his debt or no, you will be compelled to pay him all you owe him. If you owe him a pound and he owes you a million, you must pay him the pound

whether he pay you the million or not. . . . If, owing you love,
he gives you hate you, owing him love, have yet to pay it.[2]

That is a truly joyful and liberating way to live. Your mind
is set; your path is clear; you need not depend on the reactions
of others to determine how you will react to them because you
have already made your choice. Grace takes the initiative to live
with passion and compassion; it does not play it safe, but lavishes
itself on others, just as grace is daily lavished on us.

Can you imagine how the world would be transformed if
we all chose to live with gracious, generous hearts? Can you
imagine the peace we would encounter if we set aside our petty
differences and narrow-minded prejudices and embraced one
another as we have been embraced by Christ? This kind of living
would transform everything it came in contact with. Consider
the woman who broke her jar of expensive perfume over the
feet of Jesus. Even though she was criticized by others for the
recklessness of her act, Christ reprimanded her critics, telling
them they did not understand what she had done. There is no
better moment to pour your love out on another. *Carpe diem*:
seize the day!

I treasure my volumes of the collected sermons of Charles
Spurgeon, who spoke about grace with such depth and simplicity.
He described returning home one evening after a very busy day
when he was suddenly confronted by the text, "My grace is sufficient for thee." He thought about the words for a while, and
then their meaning came to him in a new way: "*My* grace is sufficient for thee." He said he burst out laughing, it was so clear. "It
seemed to make unbelief so absurd," he wrote.

It was as though some little fish, being very thirsty, was
troubled about drinking the river dry, and Father Thames

said, "Drink away little fish, my stream is sufficient for thee" . . . Little faith will bring your souls to heaven but great faith will bring heaven to your souls.[3]

All we have to do is humble ourselves before God. As we move toward Him, we will see Him running to meet us. We may feel incredibly unworthy (and we are), but we must remember that God loved us so much "he gave his one and only Son, that whoever believes in him shall not perish but have eternal life" (John 3:16).

Everyone's story is different. Perhaps you have been told you should never have been born, that you were a mistake. Perhaps you were told you would never amount to anything. So many things that happen to us as children leave greasy fingerprints on our souls. Children who have been beaten feel at some level that they deserve their beatings; those who have been sexually abused become accustomed to equating anything sexual with "love." Yet Jesus said He came to give us abundant life, life running over at the edges, more than we could ever imagine.

When you step out from the shadows into the storm, you may be at the mercy of the wind for a while, but Christ is Lord over the wind and the storms, and you will be truly alive—not just a whisper of who God called you to be. There is so much more to life than mere survival! God wants you to *live*, not just get through one more day. We can try in vain to fix ourselves, but only the One who made us knows the path to healing.

I will keep you and will make you
    to be a covenant for the people . . .
to open eyes that are blind,
    to free captives from prison
    and to release from the dungeon those who sit in darkness.

                                        (Isaiah 42:6–7)

When you find yourself at an emotional crossroads, you have to choose whether you will push your emotions down one more time, dismissing them as lightly as a summer cold, or will you stop and listen and ask God to help you understand why your life is so painful? Perhaps, like me, you will find things out about yourself that are disappointing. I, for instance, am learning to distinguish between healthy shame that alerts me to areas of my life that need to change and the unhealthy ocean of shame that does not belong to me. At times you may be overwhelmed with sadness, but if you are willing to sing its song for a little while, a great burden will be cut from you and roll down the mountain.

> *Lord Jesus,*
> *Your love for me is beyond my understanding.*
> *I am so ashamed of what I bring to You today—*
> *my fears, my shame, my hopelessness.*
> *Today I choose to come out of the shadows*
> *into Your light,*
> *into Your healing,*
> *into Your hope,*
> *into Your life.*
> *Amen.*

Farewell Lesson

I end this chapter on shame with a scene that took place on my last day of inpatient care in the hospital. I had made great strides in learning who I was in Christ and the truth of what led me to sink into a dark depression, but I still had a long way to go.

I was sitting outside with my group enjoying an unexpected Indian summer day. Our staff group leader spoke up. "Sheila is leaving us today, and I want you all to give her some input as to what you perceive her strengths to be."

I could have died! I was very uncomfortable with the idea that everyone was expected to say something nice about me. I stared at my feet.

"You seem a little uncomfortable with this, Sheila," she said. "Why?"

"Well, you are forcing people to find something good about me. It seems a little staged."

She continued, "So, is there nothing good to say?"

"Well, sure, but I have spent so much of my life trying to make people like me . . . I guess I'm not sure I really trust their perspective," I said.

"You have sat here every day with us and listened to input about your weaknesses. You've never resisted that. I think we would like to tell you what we see in you that we really like. Is that okay?" she asked.

"I guess so," I whispered.

"I see you as strong and compassionate," someone said.

"You make me laugh!" another added.

"I find it comforting to be around you," someone said. "You have a tender heart."

It was one of the most humbling experiences of my life, to look into the faces of people with whom I had gone through so much and listen to their positive appraisals. I had spent a month looking at my weaknesses. All I had wanted to do was to confess my failures to the Lord and then go and live quietly somewhere. I saw myself working in an art gallery or an antique shop in a small, sleepy town, where each Sunday I would go and take my place in church, grateful to God that He loved me and accepted me.

The group leader interrupted my thoughts. "You need to stop trying to control what is happening around you, Sheila. Be aware of other people, and don't let your pride stand in the way

of someone being able to say, 'Thank you, you have made a difference in my life.' "

That is part of what it means to live beyond the shame profile. Not only are we able to receive kind, affirming words from
others but we are also able to extend them to ourselves. When
the enemy drags old stuff out of the trash—anxiety, disappointment, despair, bitterness—and tries to paste those labels on us
again, we can refuse to wear them and stand on the rock-solid
truth that in Christ all things are made new. That is the road I
set out to travel. For years I had denied that shame had a choke
hold on my life, but till the day I die and beyond, I will thank
God that He allowed me to finally see the shame for what it is
and walk away from it.

> *It keeps me walking on the line;*
> *it holds me to the flame,*
> *yet makes me smile as if*
> *my blistered flesh can feel no pain.*
> *It pulls me far away*
> *from those whose hands I long to hold;*
> *it keeps me safe;*
> *it keeps me winter cold.*
> *So now I choose to walk away*
> *from what I know so well.*
> *I leave behind this Judas seed*
> *and all the lies I tell,*
> *and as I stand with empty hands*
> *upon this valley floor,*
> *I ask, dear Jesus,*
> *walk me through this door.*

Silence.
I hear my breath,
but nothing else.
The world is quiet.
I am alone.
Someone turned the lights out
and everyone went home.

Chapter 7

The Longest Night

*It isn't for the moment that you are stuck that
you need courage, but for the long, uphill
climb back to sanity and security.*

—ANNE MORROW LINDBERGH

I t was so quiet. I sat in my room, covered by the silence. I
wondered if it was time to eat, but I didn't want to eat alone.
I turned on the television, forty-eight channels and nothing to
watch.

It was late Friday afternoon. I had just completed my inpatient program and was due to start what was called PHP, the
Partial Hospitalization Program. For the next two weeks I was to
stay in a local hotel and return to the hospital from 8:00 a.m. to
5:00 p.m., Monday through Friday, for further counseling and
group therapy.

Instead of leaving the hospital after lunch as planned, I lingered for a short while. Strange though it may seem, this place

that once was terrifying to me now felt safe and secure, like a second home.

I sat around in the patient lounge savoring a cup of coffee. I talked to one of the nurses for a while and discovered that she, too, had been a patient in this very unit a couple of years before. I felt as if she were giving me a gift by disclosing that she had walked where I was walking. I wandered back to my room to pack my suitcase. It was time. An older nurse came in and returned all my personal items. I looked at the hair dryer and smiled to myself at being once again trusted with this "lethal" weapon. The nurse asked if I had any suicidal thoughts. I replied that I did not. She smiled and told me she hoped I had a good weekend.

I walked into the lobby to reclaim my car keys. As I waited for the desk nurse to unlock her drawer, I looked around. I remembered that first night and the fear I had felt in being there; now I was afraid to leave. I crossed the parking lot and found my little white car. I got inside and sat for a while. I remember thinking, *I hope I can still remember how to drive!* I turned the ignition, put the car into reverse, and drove off, driving skills intact. The hospital had recommended a hotel close by, for which I was grateful.

After settling into my room on the tenth floor, I looked out the hotel window to the traffic below. It was dark even though it was still quite early, and the traffic was bumper to bumper. Washington, DC, was committed to getting home from work.

I decided I would feel better if I was a part of the sea of life outside my door, so I picked up my jacket and walked to the elevator. I wondered if I looked strange. Would people waiting with me at the elevator whisper, "I think that she just got out of *that* hospital"?

I went to the front desk and asked if there was a mall close at hand. The receptionist gave me directions, and I went out to my car. My mother would arrive from Scotland in a couple of days, but for now—for a weekend—I was on my own.

I didn't know anyone in DC, and I had not told anyone in Virginia that I was "out." I had not, in fact, talked to anyone at *The 700 Club* since I had left. I felt very vulnerable. One of the women in my group was staying at the same hotel, but she had plans to be with friends that first night and I did not want to "gate crash" her time.

I felt out of my element in the outside world. I parked as close to the busy mall as I could and wandered in. People seemed to be falling over one another to get to where they wanted to be. I bought a cup of *real* coffee from a gourmet store; no more decaffeinated for me. I was back in the big world, and I needed it fully leaded. I sat and watched the men, women, and children who scurried past me: frustrated husbands who found themselves engulfed once more in a shopping frenzy; children who wanted to stop and take in the full joy of some novelty that caught their eye but who were hurried on by their parents. Suddenly I felt painfully alone. I looked into the eyes of a woman who seemed to be carrying the weight of the world on her shoulders. I wondered about her life, and was saying a quiet prayer for her when I realized someone was talking to me.

"Sheila, we are so pleased to see you. We've been praying for you."

I looked up at a woman in her forties who was smiling as she talked.

"This is my husband, Bill, and we watch *The 700 Club* every day, don't we, Bill?" Bill agreed. "How are you, dear?" she asked.

"I'm doing much better than I was a month ago," I said.

"We're so glad. We'll keep you in our prayers. Hope to see

you back on the air in no time." She reached over and hugged me, and they were gone.

I found the nearest bathroom, locked myself in, and cried. I didn't know why I was crying. I just felt more alone after they left. I wished I could have sat down and had dinner with them, to be with someone, to share a sense of closeness, of community. I dried my eyes and decided to head back to the hotel. Being in the mall made me feel too lost in the crowd.

As I pulled out of the mall entrance onto the highway, I was suddenly afraid, as if I had forgotten how to drive at night. All sorts of thoughts crashed in on me. I love to drive, it is a passion of mine, but all the lights and the noise around me seemed dark and threatening. I didn't get very far before pulling into a McDonald's parking lot to gain my bearings. As I sat there with rain beginning to fall on my windshield, I reminded myself that I was not alone; God was with me. Though I knew the words were true, I still felt cold inside.

Back in my hotel room, I sat at the desk for a long time, with my Bible open, its pages staring up at me. I felt as if I were standing on the edge of a wasteland that stretched out endlessly before me. The last month had been a fight to find my balance again. But the journey was just beginning. I was coming to grips with the impact my father's death had had on my life, and I was beginning to understand the subsequent choices I had made, but where did that leave me now?

While I was grateful for the lessons I was learning, and, in a sense, the storm had passed, I now sat in the aftermath, looking at the devastated landscape, wondering what would become of my life. I knew that it could never be "business as usual" again. Even though I was touched by the kind and hopeful words of the couple in the mall who expected to see me back on the air very soon, I knew returning there would not be right for me or for *The 700 Club*. I was beginning to heal, but I had a long way to go.

It seemed as if the road ahead was dark and lonely. I could not see how far it stretched; all I knew was that it was the only way home.

I slept late on Saturday morning and then watched old black-and-white movies on American Movie Classics. I didn't leave the room all day.

Sunday morning I decided I would go back to the church where God had spoken powerfully to me. I wanted to hear His voice again. As I got dressed, I felt a surge of hope. It was normal to feel a little dissociated when you are released from a hospital, I told myself, particularly when you have been surrounded by a loving, caring staff—brothers and sisters in Christ.

In the sanctuary I sat in the same place as before, but I didn't see anyone I recognized. I had remembered the singing as being warm and strong; now it seemed lifeless. I listened hard to the pastor's sermon, trying in vain to hear God speak to me.

When the service was over, everyone filed out, heading off to a family lunch or home to watch a ball game. I stayed and sat for a while, looking at the beautiful stained glass windows. Last time the sunlight had danced through them; now they were dull and quiet.

As I walked to my car I felt chilled all over. I had nothing to do until eight o'clock the next morning, and I didn't want to go back to my room and spend the whole day there again, so I drove downtown to Union Station. I sat in a little café, watching the people walk by. I tried to ignore my thoughts, but they would not go away. *This is your life now, Sheila. This is how it will be—alone, disconnected, devoid of purpose.*

I felt as if the hospital had given me a false picture of what was real. Of course I felt loved there; that was their job. Of course they listened; they were paid to listen. But that time was coming to an end, and now I would be all alone.

Why had I felt nothing in church? Where was God? Perhaps it was different from the last time because I was of no use to Him anymore. I knew He still loved me and that I would be with Him one day in heaven, but for now He seemed far away. I thought again of all my lofty declarations of faithfulness to the Lord, of how I would never let Him down, and how here I was, alone and silent. I had no idea what I would do. All my life I had trained and prepared for only one thing, to serve God—that was my life.

Unable to think too far ahead, I sat in the Union Station coffee shop and prayed, asking the Lord to show me where I should go now.

Other Travelers

In the real dark night of the soul it is always three o'clock in the morning.

—F. Scott Fitzgerald, *The Crack-Up*

The phrase "dark night of the soul" is the title of a beautiful work written by St. John of the Cross, a sixteenth-century church reformer who dedicated his life to calling people back to a life of obedience and prayer. He was regarded as a radical, was arrested and imprisoned, and yet the effort to silence him gave birth to his loudest and most enduring cry. In prison he wrote *The Dark Night of the Soul*, in which he described his experience of being led by God to a place where, in love, the Lord "wounds" him. Based on this experience, John of the Cross saw that God's divine plan leads us to a place where, through the pain of our broken lives, we are ready to change to become more like Christ.

Imprisonment, for this reformer, wasn't the end of the road, but the beginning of his journey.

Many of the most inspiring books and illuminating lives have been born out of what we would call tragedies. The common thread woven throughout these stories is that in the midst of their pain, the men and women reached for the hand of the Shepherd of their souls. Perhaps, like me, you can remember praying to be more like the Lord. But when life began to shake, it seemed as if you were losing ground rather than getting closer to heaven.

As I read through the pages of *The Dark Night of the Soul*, I was amazed at the places that made me stop and say, "Yes, that's right. That's exactly how I feel." To use the words of Charles Dickens, John was saying that this dark night was, for him, "the best of times" and "the worst of times." He talked of the pain and the loneliness that sat with him, and yet he was deeply aware that this was a place to which God had led him. Many different roads can lead to this same dark night. When you find yourself there, it does not matter what brought you to your knees; what matters is that you are there.

In hindsight, I believe that the way home for all pilgrims is through this bitter wasteland. It is there, when all help and all hope are gone, that we finally learn to trust in the only One who can teach us how to live. We arrive at this rusted, uninviting gateway through many different circumstances—some out of our control and some that we have brought upon ourselves. But if our trust is in Christ, He will pilot us through the deepest valleys and we will never be the same again.

Of the Bible's countless examples of those who faced their own dark night and left a little light for us to see by, none is more poignant than the life of Christ. Christ had never needed

His friends more than He did in Gethsemane, but they slept through His brow-bloodied prayers. His anguished cries to His Father pierced the night, but the world slept through His sorrow. He had no shoulder to cry on, no hand to hold, no one to comfort Him. As He was nailed to a wooden cross at the place of the skull, He cried out the greatest fear of us all, "My God, my God, why have you forsaken me?" (Matthew 27:46).

Job is another example of living in the valley, and in this man's case, his life was turned upside down for no apparent reason.

The darkness hit him with no warning. I used to find it so hard to understand why God would allow Satan to torment a man like Job. He lived a good life; not just a casually good life but a life committed to honoring God. He lived with acute intentionality. "This man was blameless and upright; he feared God and shunned evil" (Job 1:1).

Surely it is the whole point of our lives to fear God and to honor Him, but God wanted something more from Job. In one day, he lost everything. Job's response to this catastrophe? "The LORD gave and the LORD has taken away; may the name of the LORD be praised" (Job 1:21).

But Job's troubles were not yet over. He then broke out in sores from the top of his head to the soles of his feet. His wife asked him why he did not curse God and die. Job responded that we cannot accept good from God and not trouble.

When the dust had settled in Job's life, as is true with anyone, the real battle was just beginning. For a short time after tragedy strikes, we are borne along by the pace of events. When the volcano is in full force, it is an awesome sight. But when the lava dries and the white ash settles, it is deathly still. The cold, gray blanket of winter settled onto Job's shoulders.

When you look at the response of Job's friends, it's amazing to see how little has changed over the years. They had no idea what Job was experiencing. The only thing they brought to their suffering friend was words, which they tossed his way to see if any would stick. Their impatience with him is obvious; he was disturbing the quiet of their waters, and they wanted life to be back to normal as soon as possible.

Before I was admitted to the hospital, I cleared my calendar of any commitments in the months ahead. I was booked to sing and speak at a women's conference nine months away; I called the woman in charge and told her I was very sorry, but I would not be able to come. She was very upset. I apologized for any inconvenience I was causing and offered to refund any money she had already spent on promotion. Apparently that wasn't the problem; she just wanted me to come. I tried to explain what was happening to me—that I was being admitted to the hospital the next day. She answered, "You do not need to do that. I will pray for you now, and then you will be able to be with us and testify to the fact that God healed you."

This woman was just not hearing me. When confronted with an inconvenient situation that clashed with her theology and her plans, she wanted it to change. I was in such distress that I couldn't think of what to say to her. But I didn't have to say anything. She concluded the conversation by telling me she would make a few phone calls to see if I was telling the truth.

When people are in pain and at the beginning of the longest night of their lives, an endless barrage of words like those from Job's friends and those I received from this woman is like thunder in the desert: a loud and comfortless noise.

Probably the most damaging counsel offered to Job came from the young man Elihu. He basically told Job that his life made no difference. He pointed out that God is God, Job was a man. Whatever happened in life happened, and there was nothing they could do. He attacked Job's commitment to integrity in the midst of his battle, saying, "If you sin, how does that affect [God]? If your sins are many, what does that do to him? If you are righteous, what do you give to him?" (Job 35:6–7).

Elihu said there was no purpose in all of Job's suffering. I imagine most of us in times of crisis have encountered similar friends or are haunted by similar doubts and fears, but we need to hold on beyond such skeptical visitors, because after they have had their say, the Lord speaks. For Job, God pulled back the curtain for a moment and gave him a glimpse of who God is. All Job could say was, "My ears had heard of you but now my eyes have seen you" (Job 42:5).

This simple statement is one of the most profound in the entire canon of Scripture. It lays out the vast difference between head knowledge and heart knowledge. I have been a student of the Bible since I was a young girl, but now I read it differently. When I was a child, I committed verses of Scripture to memory so I could carry one more Bible prize home to my mother. When I sat at my desk at CBN answering correspondence, I would scan the pages to find a verse that seemed to fit each letter I received. But now I knew the words that were life to me, my bread and water and air, were: "I know that my redeemer lives, and that in the end he will stand on the earth" (Job 19:25).

Even as I reread the story of Job during the weeks that followed, I still found myself asking why. I know Job's story has a happy ending, but the cost attached to the lesson he learned was immense. I thought of my friend Debbie who had been struggling for so long with cancer and was now in constant pain. What could I say to her? I did not feel that I could tell her, "Hang in there. It gets better in the end."

I felt as if I were a child again, starting at the very beginning, asking the most basic questions: "What is the purpose of my life? How do I walk in the will of God? How do I live in a way that makes God happy? What does God want of me? What does it *look* like to be a Christian?"

As I entered this new phase of treatment—and of life—God was painfully silent. When I prayed, I understood what people meant when they said it seemed their prayers went no higher than the bedroom ceiling. Still, I kept praying, and I kept reading the Psalms out loud; it was all I knew to do. David had walked this path before me and had experienced the absence of God. His prayer became my prayer. I prayed out my loneliness. I prayed out my fear and anger. I prayed out the agony of being a fragile, flawed human being.

Dark Night Exposes Sin

In *The Dark Night of the Soul*, John of the Cross clearly laid out what he believed to be God's purpose in turning out the lights. It is to expose our sin, including the following elements of sin, which I saw in my own life.

Pride

John of the Cross talked about the initial "heady" days of faith, when we are overwhelmed with the love of God and passionately committed to sharing that with others. There is, he said, a tendency to judge other people and elevate oneself in the secret places of the heart. I identify with that indictment; I remember those days well. I used to love it when people would tell me that I had a remarkable ministry.

While that kind of comment should have brought me to my knees before God, it just made me feel a little more invincible. At times I had longed to get help for my life, but the price was too high; I too highly valued the respect and recognition I was given. It was as if I had a compulsion to teach and an unwillingness to be taught. Insidious pride disguises itself to look admirable on the outside, while inside, a little worm begins to grow.

Spiritual Greed

Like an addict who craves a bigger and better high, the believer craves more intense religious feelings. It is wonderful to feel the presence of the Lord, but our commitment needs to be out of obedience to Him, rather than because it makes us feel good. When we live our lives as if God exists for us—to make us happy—we have missed the point completely. Our childish behavior is based on emotional thrills. What does that self-indulgent euphoria have to do with Calvary? The whole purpose of our lives is to glorify God, to say with every fiber of our beings that we exist for Him.

When I felt my life starting to shake, I looked for some *experience* that would deliver me from my trouble. I crammed my mind with books and messages in a frantic search of a touch from heaven. I never thought to stop all my *doing* and listen. John said that out of love for His children, God will take our lives and purge them in the dark fire.

John of the Cross wrote, "For a soul will never grow until it is able to let go of the tight grasp that it has on God."[1]

This almost sounds blasphemous, and yet I understand a little of what he means. So often we cling more to our theory of who God is than to who He really is as He has revealed Himself in Christ and through His Word. I am grateful for the wonderful books and other resources available to help us in our walk with

God, but too often they take the place of God's Word; we ingest the opinions and experiences of men or women who no doubt love the Lord, but whose words should never take the place of scriptural revelation.

No matter how gifted any of us are as communicators, we are all followers, all servants, all seekers, and God is the only truth on which we can stake our lives. We are told to make our requests known to God, to ask and keep on asking, but we should always ask in an attitude of humility and awe, not demanding that He live up to our feel-good television commercials.

Anger and Disillusionment

As we face the sin of our spiritual greed, we are often confronted with anger toward and our disillusionment with God. Many times, when God calls us to "grow up" as Christians, we respond like petulant children who do not want to be weaned from their mother's breast. When it seems as if God has left us and no longer answers our prayers, we may become angry and disillusioned. John of the Cross said this frustration with our situation is not true humility, which waits for God, demanding nothing, surrendering the desire to become a "saint in a day."

Over the years I have received many letters from Christians who are disappointed in God. A lot of teaching presents Him as a benevolent sugar daddy in the sky, and when our lists of requests do not materialize, we pout as if He had failed to live up to some agreement that we ourselves dreamed up. It requires little faith or commitment to follow someone who sits with a magic wand, awaiting our bidding. That is not who God is. When prayer no longer brings feelings of heaven, when God's Word stares silently from the page, the disillusioned disciple walks away like a disappointed fan whose team is in a slump.

Dark Night and Surrender

God in His mercy, out of a desire for a real relationship with us, will continue to allow us to fall flat on our faces until all we want is Him. He is so committed to our spiritual health and growth that He will do whatever it takes to free us from our selfish nature. But this is no mindless, barbaric endurance test. He knows us well and loves us lavishly.

God's purposes are for our good, never for our destruction. We have the comfort of knowing that God, who created us, who knew us before we were born, and who perfectly knows us, has promised us that He will not permit us to be given more than we can bear. "He will not let you be tempted beyond what you can bear. . . . He will also provide a way out so that you can endure it" (1 Corinthians 10:13).

This is a concrete promise: at the right time, God will say, "It is enough." In the midst of the most painful times, I really wondered if that verse was true. I honestly believed what was happening to me *was* more than I could bear, and I wondered if God had forgotten me. It seemed that if one more thing were laid on my back—even a feather—I would break. But our God is good. As C. S. Lewis said in *The Lion, the Witch and the Wardrobe*, our Lion-King is not necessarily *safe,* but He is good.

In the dark night when no one is watching, we are given the opportunity to face ourselves and surrender wholly to Christ. I have heard many sermons on the subject of surrender; I have sung many songs that speak of little else. But what does it really mean? For me, it meant walking away from everything I loved, because I had lost touch with Jesus, the one whom I am called to love.

I had to come to a point of asking myself, "Does God exist

for me or do I exist for Him?" The answer was and is very clear. I exist to love and serve God. He does not owe me a thing, but I owe Him everything.

One of the most inspiring works I have ever read is *The Imitation of Christ* by Thomas à Kempis. Although he completed this book in 1427, the wisdom and humility displayed within its pages are utterly relevant to life today. Referring to the times in our lives when everything is dark, when there is a desolation of spirit, he said:

> It is no great thing to despise the comfort of man, when the comfort of God is present. But it is a great thing, and indeed a very great thing, that a man should be so strong in spirit as to bear the lack of both comforts, for the love of God and for God's honor should have a ready will to bear desolation of spirit and yet in nothing to seek himself or his own merits.[2]

During this dark time I saw how strong my will is. I like to be in control; I feel too vulnerable if I am not calling the shots. But now I found myself in a place where obedience—not what made me feel good—was all that mattered. As I read *The Imitation of Christ*, I saw that it was not for me to question what God was doing in my life or how long that process would take. In my younger years, it had been relatively easy for me to fast for extended periods of time or to pray and work intensely with great self-discipline. Now I saw that God wanted my heart and mind as well as a focused vision. It is spiritual suicide to throw oneself into the work of God, only to forget the face of God. Step by step, I surrendered the tight hold that I had had on my life for so long.

As I continued as an outpatient at the hospital, it became clearer to me that fear made me clench my fists. I sat in sessions with my therapist and listened as my mother talked about her own dark night. She described the darkest night of her journey, when it seemed as if the very powers of hell came into her bedroom to torment her. All sorts of sickening thoughts tore through her mind as she faced the reality of losing the man she loved and of raising three children by herself. In the midst of this attack, one "dart" bounced off her shield of faith. The voice said to her, "You are all alone in the world tonight. No one is praying for you."

My mother knew that could not be true. She knew that her grandmother, a great saint of God, would never have gone to sleep without getting down on her knees on her granddaughter's behalf.

As I sat and listened, I saw my mother's faith rise again, even as she told her story. I realized that in the midst of the worst agony of her life, she did not forget who she was. Her identity as a child of God, descended from a long line of godly people, charted her through the pitch dark of night.

One evening we sat in a restaurant and talked about the future. I had no idea what to do. Everything I had been involved in for the previous ten or twelve years revolved around a stage, and I did not believe that long-term healing could occur in a spotlight. Surface wounds heal quickly, but deeper wounds take time. So much of my life had been built around my career, and now that landscape seemed decimated.

That evening, with tears running down my cheeks, I prayed a very simple but life-changing prayer: "Father, I kneel before You now with empty hands. Whatever You put in my hands, I will welcome, and whatever You take away, I will gladly let it go."

The first step—the prayer—was relatively easy. Walking it out daily is what would prove difficult. When I fail, I am grateful for the mercy and forgiveness of God. And I am learning that because I am so strong willed, it is important for me to surrender to God without a barrage of questions—to *choose* to obey as an act of will.

C. S. Lewis described surrendering ourselves to God as the difference between looking *along* a beam of light and looking *into* a beam of light. In a book of essays titled *God in the Dock*, he told of this experience as it happened to him while sitting in a toolshed. He was watching a shaft of sunlight pouring through a crack in the wood. It was the only thing he could see—everything else was dark—until he stood up and looked through the beam. Then everything was changed; he could not see the beam at all, and yet the scene outside the woodshed was illuminated.

We can choose to live in the darkness, observing life from the safety of the sidelines, or we can step into the light and be given a bigger vision. Lewis faced his own time of agony and despair. The movie *Shadowlands* portrays something of that path of broken glass Lewis was to walk upon in the latter years of his life. He was a brilliant writer and apologist who spoke eloquently on many issues of faith, but his own taste of suffering changed his paradigm forever. In the movie we see him standing at a lectern giving a masterly speech on the purpose of suffering. The delivery was brilliant, but detached.

Then Lewis lost his wife to cancer. In the midst of his pain, it seemed to him that God was not listening, as if a door were slammed in his face "and all that I could hear was the sound of bolting and double bolting."[3] In time he spoke as one who had walked through the valley of the shadow of death. It seems as if that is the way: at first there is the cry in the darkness, "My God, my God, why have you forsaken me?"

Lewis called pain "God's megaphone."[4] Rather than being evidence that God does not care, pain is overwhelming evidence that He does. When Lewis looked *along* the beam of suffering, he spoke with eloquence. After he had stood in the place of suffering and the beam had hit him, he spoke with compassion and grace.

I recently read an interesting modern parable that spoke to this issue of darkness as a teacher. In his book *Healing the Shame That Binds You*, John Bradshaw wrote of a man who was sentenced to die and placed in a dark cave. He was told that there was a way out, and if he could find it in thirty days, he would be free. High above him, there was a small hole through which food was lowered to him every day. The man spent every waking moment trying to build a pile of stones high enough to climb to the top, to that tiny shaft of light, but by the time that he was close to the opening, he was exhausted from his efforts and fell to his death.

If the prisoner had only known that one of the stones in the side of the cave, about two hundred feet from him, had been pushed away, he could have escaped with little difficulty. Bradshaw concluded, "He had so completely focused on the opening of light, that it never occurred to him to look for his freedom in the darkness."[5]

It takes time to hear God in the darkness. It will take quiet, and quiet is a gift. "In repentance and rest is your salvation, in quietness and trust is your strength" (Isaiah 30:15). None of us would seek pain in our lives, but when you find yourself in a bleak place, it is time to pay attention to what God would say to you in the darkness. You might be surprised by what He will show you about your life. I know I was.

It is dark, Lord.
I feel so alone.
I am like a boat that is lost at sea.
I know that You are with me;
chart me through this long, dark night.
Amen.

You hold the scales of justice
so tightly to Your chest;
I wish You'd lay them down
and let me rest there on Your breast.

Chapter 8

Forgiveness Comes Full Circle

Be kind and compassionate to one another, forgiving each other, just as in Christ God forgave you.

—Ephesians 4:32

Let me describe for you my idea of a perfect evening. It's cold outside, possibly raining. A hearty fire burns in the fireplace. It crackles and dances. My three dogs snuggle up together, their white fur orange in the fire's glow.

Friends have come over, and we've had a meal that we threw together at the last moment and somehow turned out to be just right. And now we sit as close to the fire as the dogs will allow and tell stories—stories of our lives, stories we were told as children, stories born in our imaginations.

Few things are more glorious to me than storytelling. My mother has always been an avid reader. She chose to leave school when she was fifteen to help her mother with my grandfather who was ill, but her education continued through the pages of Charles Dickens and A. J. Cronin. We grew up in a small town, but in a huge world through the gift of stories. I had more than a few favorites.

I've already told you of *The Wizard of Oz* and *The Velveteen Rabbit.* And then there was *Beauty and the Beast*, which had all the "right" elements, including a lonely, beautiful heroine who faced terrible danger. Yet in the midst of this heroine's fear, she reached out to the beast, who was transformed by the power of her love.

The Ugly Duckling told a different yet similar tale. In this story, a lonely little fellow, misunderstood by others, is finally transformed into the most beautiful swan of all. Those who had rejected him are the very ones to tell him, once he becomes a swan, how magnificent he is.

The very premise of a fairy tale is that all wrongs will be righted, that good will triumph over evil, and that, in the end, truth will be revealed and the story will come full circle. It all happens within a few pages, and it all happens on this earth.

But we do not live in Hans Christian Andersen's world. We live in *this* world. As Christians, we know there will come a day when all tears will be wiped away, when peace and joy will be the only songs we know, but we have a long road to walk until that Day of the Lord. For the moment, we have to live with one another, with all the good and bad that come with it. The sad truth is that we will let one another down. We will bruise each other. We will fail. So how should we live in the midst of this reality?

I talked earlier about the first days after my release from the hospital. Now I'd like to walk you through four lessons I learned on the road to forgiveness. This road carried me back to Virginia

Beach at the end of my DC program, but the lessons started years before my breakdown.

Sowing and Reaping

Sometimes when we find flaws in ourselves or in others, we find it hard to walk with one another for the duration of the journey. Too often we leave a trail of bodies behind us. I think of situations when friends of mine were in trouble, and I believed it was my duty to them and to the Lord to help pull them up by their bootstraps. Based on what appeared to be happening on the outside, I made some quick judgment calls.

If someone lets us down, often we walk away. This happened to me. What was most painful was that I knew I had done the very same thing to a friend when she needed me. She was one of my few good friends. We went on trips together, sat for hours talking over endless cups of coffee. We laughed and cried as we shared our hopes and dreams for the future. Then one day she sat me down and told me that she thought she was gay. My first question was, "Does your husband know?"

Yes, he did. I was absolutely stunned. They had always seemed like such a happy couple. My friend was taking a risk telling me, reaching out to me for some kind of support—a sign that I was still her friend.

And when she needed me most, I was not there. All I could think was, *She must be telling me because she is interested in pursuing that kind of a relationship with me.* I ran for miles. She was a friend in trouble, and I abandoned her.

Now, years later, I sat in the doctor's office in the hospital with tears rolling down *my* cheeks. I felt crushed and thrown away.

"What is on your mind, Sheila?" he asked.

"I thought these people were my friends," I said. The people I was speaking of were those who had just walked away from me when my life had started to unravel. They were the people who had put an unsympathetic twist on my breakdown. I thought of the man who pulled me aside before I left and suggested Satan was using me to attack CBN. Once I entered the hospital, more rumors had begun flying. The evangelical world is a fairly small place, and news, especially bad news, travels fast. Bits and pieces of these rumors had been getting back to me, and I was stunned by them. All of them were untrue: from "she's had an affair" to "she's been hallucinating and seeing flying things." And some people—friends—believed these stories without even talking to me.

"I can't believe some of the things that are being said about me by people who know and love me. It makes me wonder if we were ever friends at all."

I was angry and I was hurt, but I did not know what to do. I knew that God had brought me to the hospital to give me an opportunity to look at my life and make some changes. It was hard enough dealing with what was true without trying to extinguish false fires.

The doctor said, "Why don't you go back to your room and talk to the Lord about this. Write out how you feel."

I sat down at my desk very angry. I wrote down the names of the people who had most hurt me. As I sat there, another name came to mind: the friend I had walked away from. I tried to push that thought away; that was not the point of today's exercise, or so I thought. But it became very clear to me that my reaction to her was *exactly* the point. I tried to reason it away—our circumstances were so different—but the Holy Spirit would have none of that. The fact remained that I was now reaping in my own life what I had sown in another's life. Perhaps if I had been more gracious in the past when my friend had needed me, then I would be experiencing more grace in my own life when I needed it so badly.

At the time, my friend needed to know, as she struggled with the brokenness and pain in her own life, that she had a companion in the journey. But I had refused to be there for her. As I allowed this realization to flood over me, I was horrified by what I had done. I wrote her a letter that day, telling her that I understood now what I had done to her. I asked for her forgiveness. I knew that she might not even acknowledge my letter, but I also knew that I had to do whatever it took to confess that I had seriously wronged her.

Within a few days, she wrote back to me, forgiving me for what I had done. Her letter was gracious and magnanimous. She truly forgave me. It was my first lesson in forgiveness.

The Mercy

A second lesson started to sink in on my second Sunday at the hospital, the day I talked about earlier when I visited a church and felt washed by an outpouring of grace.

When the pastor stood to give his message, I thought to myself that he looked as if he had weathered some storms of his own. I sat up and paid attention. He read Matthew 18:21–35, the story of the unmerciful servant. This man owed his master ten thousand talents, millions of dollars in US currency. Wanting to settle all outstanding accounts, the master asked his servant to repay what he owed. When the man was unable to do so, the master decided to sell this servant and his wife and children as slaves to recoup some of his loss.

Well, the servant fell on his knees and begged for mercy. He asked for more time to make good on his loans. At this, the merciful master took pity on his servant. He didn't just grant his servant's request for more time; he forgave him the entire debt.

The servant left rejoicing, but soon ran into a man who owed *him* just a few dollars. Showing no mercy, he demanded that this man pay up immediately. When the man was unable to do so, the servant had him thrown in jail.

But that's not the end of the story. When the master heard what his servant had done to someone who owed him so little, he threw the servant in jail too—until he could repay the millions he had owed.

Jesus concluded, "That is how my heavenly Father will treat each of you unless you forgive your brother from your heart" (Matthew 18:35).

The issue uppermost in my mind that morning was my own desperate need of God's mercy and forgiveness. But a few days later as I sat in my room, the rest of the story began to visit me. It was clear to me that God was saying, "I have forgiven you for so much. I have wiped all your sins away. Because of My Son's sacrifice, you are free. Now extend that mercy to others."

I did not want to do that. I was hurt and angry, and I wanted those who had hurt me to at least acknowledge they had done so—and ask to be forgiven. But the Lord would not let me rest. I was to forgive, and I was to forgive now. "How do I do this, Lord?" I prayed. "I will just be pretending, because I don't feel anything in my heart. It will only be words."

It still seemed that God was requiring something of me. It didn't matter if it made sense to me or if I felt like doing it. In obedience to this call, I began to write down the names of the people I was angry with. As I put some of those names on paper, I found myself weeping, thinking of former times when there had been peace between us—times when things had been very different.

I could write the names down. I could even think about for-giveness. But to actually forgive them—I did not know how to do it. For that, I needed a third lesson.

Forgiveness Face-to-Face

The very next day I heard a lecture on forgiveness. As I looked around the room, I realized how much harder forgiveness must be for some of the other patients than for me. Some of these women had been sexually molested by family members. How do you begin to forgive that?

Another of the women had been brutally beaten by her hus-band. What did forgiveness mean for her? She stood up and told the group that she could not forgive. It would mean everything that had happened to her was forgotten, and she could not afford to forget. The doctor told her four things:

- Forgiveness does not minimize what has been done to you.
- Forgiveness does not make the pain go away.
- Forgiveness does not blot out your memory.
- Forgiveness is a God-given strategy for dealing with the pain of life.

As I further processed what was happening in my life, I dis-covered a substantial stumbling block to my forgiving others: I found it very hard to forgive myself, so when I encountered judg-ment in others it only served to reinforce what I already believed about myself.

After my time at the hospital was over, I went back to Virginia in anticipation of my next steps. I scheduled a meeting with Pat Robertson for the following week to talk about my future with

CBN. Terry Meeuwsen, who used to fill in for me when I was on vacation, had been taking my place temporarily until a final decision was made. As I thought and prayed about the future, a new seed began to grow in me. I had spent so many years being the one who was supposed to have all the answers; now I wanted to make tentative inquiries about going to seminary. By the time I sat down with Pat, I had been provisionally accepted at Fuller Theological Seminary in Pasadena, California.

Pat offered to find me a job nearby or at Regent University. I was grateful for his offer, but told him I wanted to go back to the very basics of my faith and build a better foundation. I told Pat about going to Fuller and he was excited for me, agreeing that a couple of years away from the pressures of public life would be a wise decision.

In fact, he even asked if he could pay my way. It was one of the kindest offers I had ever received, but I declined. I wanted to take this first step of faith on my own, trusting God.

One of my coworkers at *The 700 Club* called me a few days later and told me that a reporter from the *National Enquirer* was on my tail, trying to get a photograph of me drooling or talking to ducks. I could imagine the headline: "Former Cohost of *700 Club* Seen on Beach in Bathrobe Trying to Walk on Water."

The producer of *The 700 Club* asked me to appear on the next week's show as a guest. Viewers wanted to know what had happened to me, and the *Enquirer* would be less likely to run a story if I appeared on television looking relatively normal. (The story never ran.)

I was extremely nervous as I drove through the CBN gates that morning in late November. I had done this same routine for years, but today was very different. I went upstairs to makeup. Terry Meeuwsen was in my old dressing room. I stood at the door and took a deep breath. As I walked in, the two makeup artists came over to hug me, both with tears in their eyes. It was good to see them, and they set to work. When they were finished with me, I looked at myself in the mirror and thought, *Well, if the nurse who took away my makeup could see me now!*

I walked up the familiar steps to *The 700 Club* offices and along the corridor where my colleagues had their office spaces. One after the other, they came out to hug me and tell me they had missed me. It felt so healing to be there with them, and the forgiveness that had seemed cold on paper came to life face-to-face.

There was some debate with the production team as to whether I should tell viewers that I had been in a psychiatric hospital. I was gently persuaded to say I took some time off because I was working too hard. But for me, it was a moot point. I had to tell the truth. Not doing that, I told them, put me in the hospital in the first place.

The general feeling in the production meeting that morning was that telling the truth would prompt career suicide. "Once you say what happened on air," someone mentioned, "you'll be done."

I held my ground. "This is what I need to do."

Interviews on *The 700 Club* were always live. Mine was pre-taped. I still think the production team was nervous I was going to act like a loony on live television. It was evidence that the network didn't trust me, and frankly, it hurt.

It was time to tape, so I went down to the studio. All the camera guys were there, including the floor director who had rescued me from many tough on-air situations (like the bear trainer who thought it would be easier to talk to me if he had his hand on my leg!). It was so good to see them all again.

I had prayed that morning that God would help me thank the viewers who had faithfully prayed for me—without losing it on the air. Pat was there and Ben Kinchlow, a former cohost who had rejoined the team, and Terry. It felt strange to be the one being interviewed, and yet I was very aware of the Lord's presence as I sat in that chair beside Pat. I thanked him for his love and support. I thanked those who had prayed and told them a little of what had happened to me. I told viewers that I had been diagnosed with severe clinical depression and was hospitalized and treated for it. "The doctors didn't fix me," I admitted, "but they guided me in the right direction."

I told the audience that I had been praying for some time that God would show me what the next step was, and that I was going back to school for a master's in theology from Fuller Theological Seminary in California. I relayed how excited I was about this opportunity to return to the basics of my faith and to listen and learn and grow. I ended the interview by saying how much I enjoyed being part of the ministry and thanking everyone for their support.

After I had finished speaking, Pat prayed for me, and it was all over. I left the set. I decided I liked Terry a lot, and as I've subsequently watched her, I've come to admire her strong yet tender heart. Before I left the building, one of the women I had been closest to asked to talk to me. We sat on a window ledge in the corridor. She told me she was sorry she had not been there for me; she just hadn't known what to do. How well I understood that! As we hugged and said good-bye, it was clear to us that God was working in both our lives, teaching us what it meant to love Him and each other.

I drove out of the main gates and prayed a blessing on this place in which I had learned so much. It was strange to say good-bye when it had been my whole life for so long. When I left for Washington, I had been afraid I would not be able to return, but now I was leaving freely and willingly. I left the grounds of CBN with a deeper appreciation for the gift of forgiveness that liberates all those who receive it and extend it to others, face-to-face.

In the month that followed that final appearance, I received and read more than five thousand letters from viewers telling me about their own stories. I was amazed at what I read. Letter after letter told of people struggling with their own depression or that of a loved one. I had no desire to become the poster child for depression, but I am glad that my last appearance on *The 700 Club* gave some people the courage to tell their own stories.

I am so grateful that the one thing I had thought would destroy me put me back on the road to connecting with others. My journey was just beginning.

Unbound!

The Lord showed me a fourth lesson in forgiveness. Before I left Virginia Beach to begin my new life in California, I went with a colleague to the ballet. It was a modern production, which is not usually my taste, but it had a profound impact on me. The opening dance was a depiction of a mother giving birth to her son. The dancer representing the baby stood wrapped in white cloth bandages. Other dancers began to unwrap them until the child was standing alone with one last sheath of cloth around his body. (I sense I'm losing some of you at this point!)

The boy stood there, still convinced that he was confined. Then he realized that if he took a single step, the rest of the cloths would fall away. (Fortunately he did have tights on underneath!) As I watched this performance, I had an overwhelming sense of the Lord saying, "Sheila, you are free. I brought some people into your life to start the process, but now you must walk in it."

As I began to forgive others, they returned to normal size.

I no longer saw them in monsterlike proportions. As long as I viewed someone as the enemy, I gave that person some power over my life. But as I forgave a person, I, too, was free. I saw that I could spend a lot of time imprisoned by past failures, or I could thank God for His never-ending grace and forgiveness and get on with the rest of my life.

This took me back to the lesson from Jesus' parable of the unmerciful servant. I had been forgiven much—and I was to continue to reach out to others with the grace God had offered me.

Walking in Forgiveness

Free, full, sovereign pardon is in the hand of the great King. It is His prerogative to forgive, and He delights to exercise it.[1]

—CHARLES SPURGEON

I stayed in Virginia for a couple of months before I moved to Laguna Beach. During that time, I met regularly with a wise and godly counselor who constantly encouraged me with this truth: "Jesus did not come to get you through this life. He came to live in you through this life."

This counselor helped me work through the process of responding to broken relationships. Through all the pain and confusion, I learned that everything comes to me through the merciful and loving hands of God. Knowing this seemed to shift everything, to throw open the doorway between my past and my future. This was the paradigm through which everything else in my life began to fall into place and make sense.

One of the most important steps for me was to allow anyone who felt disappointed or personally wounded by me to talk to me. My natural instinct is to stay away from what might be painful, to write people off and move on, but that is never the way of the cross. I lived that way for too long, and it is the way of the coward. I want to deal with life honestly, seeking restoration wherever possible. I used to believe that pain was a negative force that would destroy me. I do not believe that anymore.

One of the hardest things I did was to talk to a man who had hurt me through his letter, which I received just before I went into the hospital. As I drove to his home, my heart pounded in my chest. We were both a little guarded at first as we sat at his kitchen table, drinking coffee. I told him I had wanted to see him because I knew he was angry with me, and I wanted to give him an opportunity to say what he had to say face-to-face. I listened as he spoke about the confusion he experienced, as he described how helpless he felt to do anything. I told him that his letter had hurt me, but I was sorry for the pain I had caused. We only spent a couple of hours together, but the chasm between us was gone. We are friends to this day.

I accepted all those who were disappointed in me and gave them space to feel angry and wounded—even to walk away. If I knew someone had something against me, I went to them and asked them to say what was on their heart. In each case, I tried not to be defensive but to really listen and ask for forgiveness where there was a wound.

In one instance, I had hurt someone through a careless remark and knew that I had to ask for forgiveness. I hardly knew the person but had heard through the grapevine that he was angry with me. I called his secretary and asked if he would see me. We arranged a meeting for the next day. As I rode the elevator to his office, I had no idea how the meeting would go. I only knew that I had an apology to make.

I sat in a busy reception area as people rushed in and out of a maze of offices. The man came to meet me and asked me to follow him. He sat quietly, waiting for me to begin. I told him

I had come to ask for forgiveness. All sorts of excuses rumbled around in my mind, but none of them warranted utterance. I had wronged another human being, and that was all that mattered. The man was more than gracious and warmly accepted my apology. Minutes later I rode down the elevator, a humbled, grateful woman.

Whenever names or faces would come to mind, and I felt some of the old resentment stirring, I would immediately begin to pray for those people, that God's blessing would be upon them.

What happened in the weeks and months that followed was an incredible learning experience for me. I'd always been afraid of confrontation but now found it healing to sit with people where there had been a breach in relationship and listen to them, then share my own heart. Some relationships were restored and some were not—I am fine with that. I have had to take time to grieve over loss, accept it, and move on. The best gift of all, however, is that with those who continued to walk with me, no matter how rocky it got for a while, I have a depth of friendship that I never before knew was possible.

A Plea for Understanding

Today, our world is littered with broken, bitter people who need love and instead receive judgment. By love, I do not mean a soft, quiet thing, but a powerful force for good. Love breaks down and builds up. It is transforming. Judgment, however, brings condemnation and fear. It is cowardly because it distances itself from the pain of life. Rather than healing what is bent, it cripples and abandons.

True love, the love that speaks the truth and yet refuses to abandon others, gives people an opportunity to change. It even motivates them to change.

Perhaps God will bring someone to your mind as He did with me—someone who needs your love in the same way that Christ loved you. It is never too late to start again.

> *Dear Father, who forgives all our sins,*
> *who showers us with mercy and compassion,*
> *teach us to love as You love;*
> *teach us to forgive as You forgive;*
> *teach us to live as You lived.*
> *For Christ's sake,*
> *Amen.*

Part 3

The Road Home

So many nights I sat alone
weighing the emptiness,
handling this stone.
Day after day, lost in the noise,
stifle the sadness, muffle the voice,
and then the hammer fell;
it took the house as well.
Let it go, let the whole thing go.

Chapter 9

Following the Shepherd

*Men are disturbed not by things, but by
the view which they take of them.*

—Epictetus

I've read that Michelangelo was seen one day pushing a large rock down into his sculptor's "studio." His neighbors watched the ferocious effort he put into moving it, inch by inch. When one of the spectators asked him what he was doing, he replied, "I saw the angel in the marble and carved until I set him free."

I believe that God will lovingly push us inch by inch to chip away the hard edges of our lives, to refine us into works of art in which others will see His hand. Though such refining is never easy, it is what we were created for. Too often we settle for a mere existence when the hope of life in all its glory and pain is waiting inside the rock.

Just as Michelangelo's neighbors didn't see the hidden treasure before them, what we see—about ourselves, others, the past, the future—is often a matter of perspective. One night, while at a ballet, I sat behind a woman whom I thought I recognized as a friend I had not seen for a while. I couldn't wait for the first intermission so I could surprise her. As the curtain fell, I tapped her on the shoulder and said hello. When she turned around, I realized my mistake. She was a he! Seeing this person from a different angle, I realized he did not look anything like my friend. (She doesn't have a beard, for one thing!) A different angle further defined the truth. And so it is with life.

When I was eighteen, my favorite book was *Hinds' Feet on High Places* by Hannah Hurnard. It tells the story of a young girl named Much Afraid, who chooses to leave the valley of fear where she has lived for years and follow the shepherd up into the mountain. Time after time she wants to stop and go back to the valley because the road ahead looks all wrong. Whether or not she continues her ascent up the mountain depends on whether or not she will trust the shepherd. Just before I left Virginia, a *700 Club* viewer sent me a new copy of that book, and I began to read it again. Suddenly I saw myself in this young girl's position, full of fear, lacking in trust, subject to every wind blowing around her.

As I read, I took particular note of one thing: At every key point when Much Afraid chose to trust the shepherd and take one more step, the shepherd gave her a stone to keep. At the end of her long journey, when she finally "died to herself" and was given new legs to run with, she was taken—by two traveling companions, Suffering and Sorrow, chosen by the shepherd—to the top of the mountain. There she saw that each rough, colorless stone had become a beautiful jewel for her crown.

I believe that God, like the shepherd, would have us live trusting Him at every turn. It was hard for me to let go, to truly trust Christ for my every breath, but as I continue on this journey now, I know as deep as the marrow in my bones there is no other way to live. What I used to know in my head, I now know in my heart. It is one thing to believe in the ability of a surgeon to perform life or death surgery on your body; it is quite another to allow yourself to be put to sleep and submit yourself to his knife.

As we trust, God is faithful to give us the spiritual rewards outlined in Psalm 23. I have loved this psalm since I was a child when I learned to sing it to a wonderful old Scottish melody named "Crimmond."

In moving to California, I began to experience the Twenty-third Psalm in a new way. The territory was new. The road was scary. And at every turn God beckoned me to trust. He wouldn't let me down.

The Lord Is My Shepherd, I Shall Not Be in Want

As I prepared to leave Virginia Beach to attend seminary in California, it was sad to say good-bye to friends and colleagues, yet I felt anchored by a new hope I had not felt before. When you have faced the worst there is to know about yourself and experienced the gift of grace, life is new and wonderful.

On June 1, I left Virginia to drive to my new home, a pretty apartment in Laguna Beach, close to the beach. My friends were horrified that I was driving across the country by myself, but I was excited about the adventure. One friend baked enough cookies for the entire trip. Another taped herself reading stories to me, and one of my best friends (who had been Pat Robertson's security guard) gave me a baseball bat in case I ran into trouble at any rest areas! I took five days to drive from coast to coast, stopping off to see friends in Indiana and Colorado. I enjoyed every moment of the trip.

I remember those first few days in Laguna well. I had arrived two months before classes began so I could settle into my apartment. It was such a happy feeling to open the door and walk into the freshly painted shell of my new home.

I sat on the floor by the window and poured out my heart to God. I thanked Him for giving me safety on my cross-country journey and for His constant companionship. Everything was new. It was as if I had been born all over again, with only a few scars to remind me of where I had been.

Just hours later, the movers arrived with my furniture. As they brought in the boxes, I unpacked them. They teased me about all the books I had as they carried box after heavy box into the apartment. I made them lunch, and we sat down on the floor to eat. I was filled again with a sense of the dignity of human life. As we broke bread together, I wondered about their stories. It is so easy not to see people, to rush past with no eye contact, guarded and insulated from life. I thought about the men in the homeless shelter I drove past every day in Virginia Beach as I rushed to get to my "safe" studio—where no one could touch me—to talk about the love of God.

I thanked the moving men for their kindness as they left, and they shook my hand and wished me happiness. I slept like a baby that first night and woke to the sun streaming through my window.

I arrived at my new home with only enough furniture to fill a one-bedroom apartment and enough money to pay my rent and tuition for three months. In material terms, I was returning to the early days of my full-time ministry, when life had been a constant adventure of watching God faithfully provide not more than I needed and not less. Over the years I had accumulated a lot of "stuff" that demanded to be maintained. And while I knew the Lord was the giver of all that is good, I had lost that sense of depending upon Him for my daily bread.

Now I had left the "stuff" behind to live a simpler life. I remember sitting one day in my tiny living room with two white chairs and my books surrounding me. I prayed, "Well, here we go, Lord. This is it. I'm leaning on You because I have nothing else to lean on."

I still needed a few basics: a refrigerator, a washer, a dryer. I shopped around and the best price I could find was eighteen hundred dollars for the three. While that would have been nothing to me before, it now stood in front of me as a challenge. I asked the Lord to show me what to do. And He answered in a way I never expected. Before I had left for California, a friend in Virginia had asked if I would sing a song for a project he was working on for children in China. When he asked me if I had a fee, I said no, I wanted to do it simply because I believed in what he was doing.

Now, months later, I wandered down to my mailbox in Laguna, enjoying the beautiful California sunshine, and found a letter from my friend. In it was a check for eighteen hundred dollars. The Lord had provided my need—to the dollar.

Just as David had recorded in the Twenty-third Psalm, I was able to say I was not in want because the Lord was my shepherd.

He Makes Me Lie Down in Green Pastures

Each morning in my new home I walked along the beach with the water lapping at my feet. I sat with a cup of coffee and my Bible on a favorite rock, bathing in the presence of the Lord.

For me, there is always something very healing about the ocean. It speaks of the power and majesty of God, and yet as I watch it flowing gently over a rock, taking years to change its face, it reminds me of His tenderness and patience as well. As a little girl I loved the sight and sound of the ocean. I would stand at the edge and watch the tide go out, knowing it would faithfully return. That's where I was again.

I found my new, simple life quite liberating. There's something very basic about "green pastures." Sometimes, however, we aren't content with green; we want "greener." Without realizing it, I had become consumed with things, using them to fill the emptiness inside me. Now I did not need to crave things, because the dark places in my life were being filled daily by the friendship of God. As someone once said, "If the grass on the other side looks greener it's probably Astroturf!"

I spent time with a counselor, a godly older woman. Each week we would look at what a Christian woman should be—how to be strong and yet gentle. I would wake up in the morning smiling, having slept all night with no bad dreams. Just as surely as God had led me to a dark valley, He was leading me to a place of peace and restoration.

He Guides Me in Paths of Righteousness

I remember my first day of seminary classes. I was so nervous! Since the class was at night, I had all day to look forward to the unknown. I started "future tripping." What if I couldn't make the grade? One of the aspects of clinical depression is the inability to concentrate; what if I couldn't do the work? There was only one way to find out.

I arrived on campus early, in case I couldn't find the right classroom. Carrying a clean, white legal pad and three new pens, I was the first one there. I had a choice of any seat, and took one near the back.

At exactly 6:30 p.m., Professor Nathan P. Feldmeth looked up and welcomed us to a new term of study. Then he led us in a prayer of thanksgiving for the privilege to be able to study and learn and grow. The class was in early church history. "This is our history," he said. "Let us start at the very beginning of our story."

What a gift to someone who had lost her way! It might not sound appealing to some—to find yourself back in a classroom again—but I welcomed it. I was hungry to learn more about the ways of God, to rebuild my life on a solid foundation. I sat in that classroom overwhelmed by the goodness of God.

From that time on, each course I took put a piece in the puzzle for me: Christian ethics, the writings of C. S. Lewis, Paul and the church, the foundations of spiritual life. There could have been no greater gift than these classes were to me.

I worked hard and gave myself to the discipline of learning. And I had a lot to learn. When I did not know how to format a paper for a master's class, I found the professors more than willing to teach me, now that I was not afraid to be taught.

I surrounded myself with good books and good friends who shared a heart to become more like Christ. Although I was alone more than I have ever been, in the library, living alone, I was never, not even for a moment, lonely. Now that I had found my voice, I was able to ask for prayer or simply for company. As I immersed myself in the Bible, I formed a firm foundation for my life built on the character of God and not on anything I might have to offer. I felt whole. God was leading me on a new, right path.

I Will Fear No Evil, for You Are with Me

When I had visited California in April to sign up for classes, a friend had called and asked me to stay a little longer and attend a "life-changing" seminar.

"I really think it would be good for you, Sheila," she said. "It has had a tremendous impact on our lives. Please say that you will think about it." She and her husband profusely recommended this seminar that had helped them discover who they were.

I assured her I would think about it, but after we said good-bye I was not sure I wanted to go to an intense four-day conference. I was tired of making changes. I had been out of the hospital only a little more than four months, and the thought of another life-changing event was a lot to swallow. But there had been something in my friend's voice that sounded different to me, and that difference was even more pronounced with her husband. He had always seemed a little cynical, but there had been no trace of that in his voice when we had spoken on the phone.

Even though I knew very little about the content of this seminar, I decided to go. I was to be at a hotel in Anaheim, close to Disneyland, by eight o'clock on Thursday morning. The conference would run through Sunday night. If it was too much for me, I figured I would just go and ride Space Mountain.

My friends had asked me to come with an open heart, to be prepared to get some feedback about my life. I was learning to be open to feedback, but it was still a relatively new concept to me. It had been my experience that if you appeared successful, people tended to come to you for advice. They don't usually take the risk of telling you where they think you need to shift your perspective (though perhaps I gave out signals that I was not open to that kind of input).

On Thursday morning, I remember thinking to myself, *I hope this isn't a big cheerleading session where we all tell each other how wonderful we are.*

I should not have worried!

Forty of us sat in a circle. The instructor began, "This is not a seminar. This is your life. Who you really are will show up in this room at some point over the course of the next four days. You will receive from this experience exactly as much as you put in. Our purpose is to come to grips with what Christ meant when He said, 'Love the Lord your God with all your heart and with all your soul and with all your mind. . . . Love your neighbor as yourself'" (Matthew 22:37, 39).

Well, at least he uses the Bible, I thought.

The first day was spent responding to questions and choosing a team partner for the weekend. I chose a tall girl who had smiled from ear to ear since she'd walked in the door. Over the next four days, with our partners and with the larger group, we were given numerous opportunities to receive and give feedback about one another's perceived strengths and weaknesses.

A few of the lines of feedback I received included, "You seem very angry," "I see a mixture of strength and self-pity," and "You have compassion for others, but you are very wounded and you hold yourself back."

It was hard to listen to total strangers tell me my flaws. I would not recommend walking up to someone in the mall and asking what that person thinks of you, but in the context of this seminar—a controlled, supportive setting—I was willing and able to hear what was being said. I had prayed that morning that God would continue to teach me how to be more like Jesus, so I chose to stay open and not close down.

I was surprised at how accurate some of the observations were. I thought I had come *so far* in my growth, and yet I still had big strides to make. That weekend was not exactly "the valley of the shadow of death," but it was a valley of shadows. I faced many things about myself, some of what I learned in the hospital about my dark places. And in that valley I realized again the truth that God was with me.

Your Rod and Your Staff, They Comfort Me

In Scripture, the rod is always used for correction. It is portrayed as the tool God uses to discipline His children. As a child I was spanked only twice that I can remember; both times I really deserved it. Yet I knew without a doubt that my mother loved me—it was painful for her even to speak harshly to me—and I never made the same mistakes again. God does not turn a blind eye to the sin or foolishness of His children, but His discipline is just and merciful, and when it is over, if we have not stiffened our hearts in rebellion, we are changed; we look a little more like Him.

Years ago I adopted an abandoned cat from the humane society. I called him Max. When Max was brought in by someone who had found him lying by the road, he was almost dead—unconscious and covered with blood. When I saw him he had just had his stitches removed and a drainage tube taken out of his back. What attracted me to him were his eyes. He has the kindest cat eyes I have ever seen. I asked if I could hold him, and he nestled in my arms, purring like an engine. I told the nurse I couldn't believe how sweet he was, and she replied, "The ones who have been through a lot are usually the most tender."

I took Max home with me. What a joy! Then one day I noticed that he was walking with a limp, though he didn't seem to be in any pain. The vet explained that Max had torn a tendon. No, he wasn't in pain, and I had options. I could leave the leg as it was and Max would be fine, but he wouldn't be able to jump as high or run as fast as he had before. Or Max could undergo surgery and get the tendon repaired.

I thought about the pain of putting him through another operation. Would it be worth it? I decided to go for it. After all, he had given me so much joy; he deserved the best that life could offer. The surgery would be incapacitating for a short time, but then Max would be back to his former self—able to do everything he set his sights on.

I saw parallels in my own life. While it is painful to allow God to perform surgery on our hearts, every time we submit to the knife, we become a little more like we were created to be.

God often allows other people to be part of the painful process of teaching us to be like Him, but He does not take delight in the destruction of a brother or sister. It is clear that we are to hold one another accountable for our lives, but when discipline is necessary we are to do it with tears in our eyes. Because not one of us knows what tomorrow will bring, let us sow mercy in the lives of others, so that God will be merciful to us.

I painfully remember a dinner with my good friends Frank and Marlene at one of my favorite Laguna Beach restaurants. I love Indian food, and this particular place served some of the finest Indian cuisine I had ever tasted. During dinner, Frank said something I disagreed with and I told him so, strongly. After a few silent seconds, he said to me, "Do you know how it makes me feel when you talk to me like that?"

I said no.

He said, "I can't hear what you are saying because you are so angry; your anger is all I hear."

We were quiet for a while, and then I turned to Marlene and asked her what she thought. Marlene recounted a day trip the two of us had taken together and asked me if I remembered what I said to her in the parking lot. I did remember—but my version was different from hers. My recollection was that she had said something I thought was out of line, and I told her so. She said, "I agree with you that what I said was probably wrong, but I do remember how stupid it made me feel to have you talk to me in the tone of voice that you used. You were so angry and condescending with me."

It was a sobering evening. When two people I love told me the same thing, it seemed wise to pay attention. I woke up the next morning to a beautiful day. I called my counselor and asked if it would be possible to squeeze me in. Yes, she could. I told her what had happened the previous evening and that I wanted to change, but felt stuck.

During the course of the next hour and a half, this woman listened, asked questions, and provided some wonderful insight. One of the practical things she suggested was to write out the phrase "God loves a woman with a quiet and a gentle spirit." She told me to put it on my refrigerator door and pray using that verse every morning. I did that, and I believe God is helping me change.

The turning point for me was listening to the input from people I love without being defensive. I realized I was what I call a "quiet terrorist," someone who didn't look like an angry person, but who liked to quietly control things from the sidelines. I now highly value genuine feedback from close friends. People who love us want us to be the best people that we can be. Change is painful, but it gives birth to a new quality of life.

And it takes courage to confront one another in love. It is still hard for me at times to be as open as I need to be, but I work very hard at it. It is especially difficult for me to own up gently when I am upset with someone because my natural tendency is to say nothing. Of course, the anger eventually seeps out in subtle ways. I realize now that this is sin. When I harbor feelings in my heart that I don't lovingly tell the other person about, then

I am controlling the situation rather than giving that person a chance to respond.

Still, I have to choose to do this. Some lessons I've learned are easy for me to act on, but this one is not. What I remind myself of in these situations is that it is God's expressed purpose for us to walk in the light with one another, so I do it—not because it feels good, but because it is right.

Friends who confront us with our weaknesses but never build us up are like Job's comforters who tear at us piece by piece. In his book *With Open Heart*, Michel Quoist tells of hearing the news that a good, generous friend of his had died, "defeated by depression." Quoist imagines what the funeral is going to be like and knows that praise will be heaped upon the dead man and his every virtue extolled. As he thinks about that scene, he says, "The tragic thing is that just a fraction of it [while he was alive] could have perhaps saved him."[1]

We all need to hear encouragement. We need our strengths to be named and appreciated. On the other hand, friends who never speak what they perceive to be true about our sins or our failures are like tightly wrapped umbrellas that are full of holes: you think you can count on them until the rain begins to fall and you find yourself soaked to the skin. We need to love one another so actively that we speak both words of challenge and words of hope. In their book *Disciplines for the Inner Life*, Bob and Michael Benson say there is no truth toward Jesus without truth toward our fellowman. Untruthfulness destroys fellowship, but truth spoken in love cuts false fellowship to pieces and establishes genuine brotherhood.[2]

In the psalmists' day, a shepherd's staff was used as a tool to guide and to lean on. It is one thing to believe that Christ carries a staff; it is another to lean on Christ and be held up. The hooked end of a staff is used to pull a lamb back from the brink of disaster or nudge a straying lamb back on to the road, into the flock. The letter from the woman suffering with cancer that began my healing process in 1992 was, in a way, like the shepherd's staff tugging at me. God in His grace nudged that woman to let me know that she *saw* me and knew I was in pain. I still have and treasure her letter, which is a comfort to me.

David stated that he was comforted by both the rod and the staff of the Shepherd. At one time I would not have understood that, because I viewed discipline as a pain to be avoided. Now I see that discipline is surely a gift to be treasured if I want to live a life pleasing to God.

You Prepare a Table Before Me in the Presence of My Enemies

I remember vividly the moment in that weekend conference when I first learned to accept feedback about my weaknesses. In one of the final exercises, the group was asked to imagine that they were on a sinking ship. There were only two spots open on the lifeboat. Each one of us was handed a Popsicle stick and asked to give it to the one person we believed would make the greatest impact with his or her life if spared. I gave mine to a man who was determined to go home and be a better husband and father. I believed him. What I didn't expect was that almost everyone else gave their sticks to me.

I know it was just an exercise, but I did not want to be the one who survived, who was entrusted with that much faith. As far as I was concerned, those days were over. I just wanted to live quietly. One of the seminar leaders stood behind me as the numbers grew and asked me, "Are you listening?"

I was listening, but I did not know what to do with what

I heard. I thought back to a movie that has been a favorite of mine for years called *The Mission*. In this film, Robert De Niro portrays a man whose actions had led to the death of his brother. A consuming guilt eats at him like a cancer. Then he is given an opportunity to help some missionaries carry supplies to a new mission base at the top of a mountain.

The climb is brutal and bloody, but he insists on carrying all the supplies tied to his back. Each time he stumbles and slips back down the unforgiving stone face, someone offers to step in and help him carry his burden. But he always refuses and continues to drag himself to the top of the mountain. As he reaches the summit, a native Indian approaches and cuts his burden from him. As it rolls off his back, the old man looks into De Niro's face and begins to laugh. De Niro, too, begins to laugh and laughs until he cries.

There comes a time when we have to let the past go. On the cross, Christ paid for our sins. He took our load upon Himself. When we have received the grace to repent in brokenness, when we have done all that we can to right any wrong, we need to allow Christ to cut our burdens from us. We cannot be defined forever by our mistakes; rather, we need to be defined by the anointing hand of God, who calls us to worship Him and serve Him with humility.

As people placed their confidence in me that night, I knew I was loved and forgiven. But I hesitated to "hear" them, because I felt being forgiven did not mean I was ever to return to a leadership role. When I voiced that feeling to the man who stood at my shoulder, he said, "Are you insisting on being in control again, or are you willing to listen?"

I thought about what he said and realized one of my oldest fears was still at play—the fear of being rejected, of making enemies. If I simply removed myself from the game, then no one would have a chance to vote me out. I needed to stop protecting myself.

I decided, from that point on, to walk in honesty with others, knowing that some people would vote against me. If enemies rose, I would need to respond with humility, but not in fear. With a "table set before me in the presence of my enemies," I could hold my head high in the confidence of the Lord. First Peter 5:6 says, "Humble yourselves, therefore, under God's mighty hand, that he may lift you up in due time."

If others look to me to be a part of their journey—to be a leader—I do not have the right to walk away. I have to rely on the knowledge that Jesus is the one who places value on my life, no matter how good or bad others think I am.

As he lay in a Roman cell awaiting execution, Paul wrote to his friends in Philippi, "Rejoice in the Lord always. I will say it again: Rejoice! Let your gentleness be evident to all. The Lord is near. Do not be anxious about anything" (Philippians 4:4–6). Paul was in the clutches of Nero, an evil, brutish emperor who delighted in the suffering of others. History tells us Nero would hold feasts on the palace grounds and illumine the proceedings with the burning bodies of Christians. Yet Paul was not afraid of this petty potentate. He had been through the fires of suffering, and his sights were set on a land Nero could not touch.

First John 4:18 says that "perfect love drives out fear." God will do what it takes until that love is perfected in us. And as we listen, He will show us the next step in our ministry—the work He has anointed us to do—whether it is quietly singing songs to young lambs or publicly proclaiming His grace.

I've mentioned my friend Marlene. She is a constant encouragement to me to continue walking a transparent, simple life, humbly before God. One day Marlene called and asked if I would be available to speak at a women's luncheon in a country club in Palm Springs. I said no, as I wasn't a speaker. At that point my background was music and television. The thought of speaking to a crowd of women was terrifying.

Marlene persisted. I told her that it wasn't that I was reluctant to help, but I just didn't know how to do that. I reminded her that she knows almost every Christian female speaker in America. Her response has stayed with me for years! She said, "Okay, here's the deal. I've asked them all. No one can do it. You're the bottom of the barrel." So reluctantly I said yes.

When I woke up on that Saturday morning, I wanted to smack myself upside the head. "Why did I say I would do this!?" As I drove to Palm Springs, I talked with the Lord and told Him, "I would just like to apologize up front because You are not going to look good today!"

When I got to the event, it was worse than I thought. Limos drove up with women in classic Chanel suits and perfect makeup (and faces that didn't move!). I parked my non-limo at a distance and walked in. The venue was staggeringly beautiful. More than a thousand women were gathered in the ballroom, seated at exquisite tables set with the finest china and crystal. As I took in this magnificent scene, I prayed for the imminent return of Christ! I was placed at the head table beside the most beautiful woman I had ever seen. The kind of woman you stare at even though you don't mean to. Actually, the kind of woman that makes you want to cry out, "Really, Lord? Share the love a little!"

Then they announced me. I stood at the podium and shot up a desperate prayer. "What do I do now, Lord?"

In my spirit I heard Him say, "Just tell the truth."

So I did. My opening line was, "Hello, my name is Sheila, and eight weeks ago I was released from a psychiatric hospital."

That apparently tends to settle a crowd right down.

I spoke the truth. I talked about my experience in the hospital and about the grace and mercy of God as I faced my greatest fears. Apparently I struck a chord with the polished women listening to me. Tears flowed through flawless makeup. That moment was different from anything I had experienced before. This was not a motivational, faith-building speech; it was just the raw, unpolished truth. At the end of my talk I invited anyone who wanted to talk to me to join me at the front of the ballroom. The first one there was a pretty blonde who took off her gold cuffs and showed me where she had slit her wrists. I realized that some of our masks are more expensive than others but they serve the same purpose, to hide the pain.

We all stood and talked for a while. One woman told me she had been struggling with depression for years and had never told anyone. The woman beside her gave her the name of a good Christian doctor. Another told me her daughter was in a psychiatric hospital. She had never shared this with others for prayer because she felt it would stigmatize her child forever. We stopped there and then and prayed for her. I will never forget that morning. It was amazing to be part of the body of Christ in action. That experience of deep connectedness through brokenness has multiplied over and over in other situations. Rather than our wounds being our enemy, they can be the very conduits of grace and mercy to one another.

And I Will Dwell in the House of the Lord Forever

The Twenty-third Psalm ends with these words: "Surely your goodness and love will follow me all the days of my life, and I will dwell in the house of the LORD forever." What a promise! I begin each day with a prayer of thanks that I am living in the midst of God's abundant, full life. I have good friends who love me and whom I love. We speak the truth to one another and support one another. When the Lord brings to my mind something I need to deal with, I make a commitment to do so at the first possible moment. When I find old resentments coming to the surface, I stop and immediately pray for that person, asking that God's mercy and grace will visit that person in ways he or she has never known before. My life feels light.

I have known the Twenty-third Psalm since I was a child, but now I know this psalm:

> *I whisper Your name*
> *and before it sounds on my lips,*
> *You are here by my side.*
> *Too blind to see,*
> *too afraid to ask*
> *it took the loss of all I had*
> *to discover who I am.*
> *Some nights are darker than the sea bed*
>   *with no moon,*
> *but a stronger light*
> *that fits me like a baby in the womb*
> *moves me through the mist,*
> *and I would live a thousand nights without one star*
> *to know that when I whisper Your name*
> *here You are.*

This earthly life is merely the overture to our eternal life with Christ. Overtures give you a taste of what is to come, but if you left the theater after these preliminary bars of music, you would miss the masterpiece.

David was a man who trusted the Shepherd. That trust

and humility strengthened the very marrow in his bones. It is a wonderful way to live. It brings dignity and peace to the human heart. There is a poem that paints a passionate picture of the kind of man David was, the kind of woman I want to be. I would love to share it with you.

If

If you can keep your head when all about you
Are losing theirs and blaming it on you,
If you can trust yourself when all men doubt you
But make allowance for their doubting too,
If you can wait and not be tired by waiting,
Or being lied about, don't deal in lies,
Or being hated, don't give way to hating,
And yet don't look too good, nor talk too wise:
If you can dream—and not make dreams your master,
If you can think—and not make thoughts your aim;
If you can meet with Triumph and Disaster
And treat those two impostors just the same;
If you can bear to hear the truth you've spoken
Twisted by knaves to make a trap for fools,
Or watch the things you gave your life to, broken,
and stoop and build 'em up with worn out tools:
If you can make one heap of all your winnings
And risk it on one turn of pitch-and-toss,
And lose, and start again at your beginnings
And never breathe a word about the loss;
If you can force your heart and nerve and sinew
To serve your turn long after they are gone,
And so hold on when there is nothing in you
Except the Will which says to them: "Hold on!"
If you can talk with crowds and keep your virtue,

Or walk with King—nor lose the common touch,
If neither foes nor loving friends can hurt you;
If all men count with you, but not too much,
If you can fill the unforgiving minute
With sixty seconds' worth of distance run,
Yours is the Earth and everything that's in it,
And—what is more—you'll be a Man, my son!

—RUDYARD KIPLING

Master strokes across a faceless canvas—
bold moves, color splashes over stones,
unfettered, young, full of dreams.
Beneath His brush the impossible comes to life,
awesome and intimate.
I stand amazed, silenced by the gift;
then He dips my finger in the paint
and I become part of the picture.
I feel so small.
It's like finger painting with Picasso,
but as God takes my hand
the paint on His melds with mine.
A new color is born.

Chapter 10

New Beginnings

*Sometimes, reaching out and taking someone's
hand is the beginning of a journey. At other
times, it is allowing another to take yours.*

—VERA NAZARIA

The first few months in California were a blur of taking classes and slowly and carefully broadening my circle of friends. I wasn't quite sure what the future held once I graduated, but frankly that wasn't my concern. At one point I considered going to India to work with Hulda Buntain, a woman I had interviewed on *The 700 Club* who worked with orphans in Calcutta. Dating was definitely the furthest thing from my mind.

When I had been in seminary for six months, I received a phone call from Barry, the head of programming at a national Christian network headquartered in California. He wanted to know if I'd consider hosting my own talk show. I was still in seminary at the time, and though I was leaning toward no, I agreed to meeting Barry at the studio.

I arrived wearing my signature ensemble, a black pencil skirt, a black T-shirt, and a black soft leather jacket. As I walked through the door, I realized I had no idea what Barry looked like. I peered around the maze of wires, monitors, and bulky video cameras as people carrying clipboards and wearing headsets hurriedly brushed past me without so much as a glance in my direction.

Suddenly my eyes fell on a handsome man sporting a stark white shirt and a tie under a beautiful and tailored Italian suit. I had never been someone who was struck giddy by the sight of a good-looking man, so I was shocked when my knees got a little weak. Mr. Handsome returned my gaze and smiled. When he started walking over to me, my stomach knotted like a pretzel. "You must be Sheila," he said with a smile. "I'm Barry." Imagine my surprise.

We chatted for a bit, and I asked if he could point me toward the makeup room so I could touch up my face. "Sure," he said and walked me to his office, which I thought strange. Barry told me later that he was immediately drawn to me and was so nervous he had no idea what he was doing.

I stood in front of a tiny mirror on his wall reapplying my lipstick while Barry sat in his chair making small talk. It was obvious we enjoyed each other's company. While the conversation flowed smoothly, I still found it awkward to be putting on makeup while he watched. If he hadn't been so attractive, I probably would have excused myself on the spot.

At some point, a bunch of noisy thirtysomething men wearing suits and ties barged in. "Let's go, dude, we're going to be late for your birthday dinner," one of them groaned. "We can't lose our reservations." Barry told them to give him a minute and stuck around talking to me for a few more. I felt flattered.

Our connection was blatant, and though we had talked a lot that evening, Barry didn't mention seeing each other again. In fact, I was leaving the next day for a ten-day trip to Scotland. I figured if he wanted to call, he had my number. He seemed smart enough to figure out the math.

Ten days later I flew back to the States, anxious to get off the bumpy flight and find out if Barry had called or not (no cell phones back then!). When I got home, I frantically checked my answering machine. I had thirty-two calls. I fast-forwarded through every voice mail that wasn't from Barry. My heart sank as I got through the middle of my messages and I hadn't yet heard from him. By the time I got to the last call, I was truly disappointed. *Maybe my radar was off from too much pizza the night before. Maybe I only imagined our connection.*

I hit the Play button for the last message. And there it was—Barry, asking me out to dinner. I had sensed a slight twinge of nervousness in his voice. He told me later he didn't want to sound desperate and chose to call me on the last day of my trip.

Our first dinner led to others, and before we both knew it—and much to my surprise—we started dating. The more I got to know Barry, the more I liked him. Besides him being drop-dead gorgeous, he was funny and made me laugh. He listened as much as he talked. And hailing from South Carolina, he wooed me with his Southern charm.

Barry didn't know much about my past—as a matter of fact, when the network asked him to call me, all he knew about me was that I was a well-known cohost from *The 700 Club*. I was an open book and shared with him about my depression. Over late-night dinners and long walks on the beach, we talked about where we had been, what we had gone through in life. But our relationship wasn't focused on our past; we cared about and enjoyed each other in the present.

Falling in love was both wonderful and terrifying. Wonderful for obvious reasons, but terrifying because this journey was so new, and I was unaccustomed to feeling safe and happy. I was just beginning to put life back together again, and I wasn't sure I could trust myself. It took me a long time to rebuild a sense of identity, to believe that I was not a crazy person but that I had a treatable mental illness.

I had worked hard to believe I was able to make good decisions, but the dizzying power of falling in love with an incredible man resurfaced the self-doubts. I broke up with Barry on three separate occasions, only to miss him like crazy, talk about what was going on in my head, and resume where we left off.

That's the thing with internal issues. Some of them don't just go away. They return every so often and force you to rethink certain things, for better or for worse. I pressed through my self-doubts, but it was still hard to trust myself.

For years I had trouble naming what I was feeling, though I could easily target the pulse of what was going on with other people.

I remember working with a therapist in the hospital. During one of our sessions, he held up a chart with a list of emotion words like *angry, scared, vulnerable.*

"Which one of these are you feeling?" he asked.

"None." I shrugged. "I'm not feeling any of them."

The therapist pressed further, asking me to really think about the question, dig deeper. Still nothing.

Finally, as he continued to pepper me with questions to draw something out of me, I snapped. I shot up out of my chair and hurled it across the room. As it bounced noisily on the floor, I glared at him and blurted angrily, "Will that work for you?"

He smiled. "Yup! That's a great place to begin."

Learning to trust myself was a process I continued after

moving to California. My new therapist helped separate what were genuine feelings versus shame-based responses from issues of my past. Part of the learning curve was understanding the residual effects of the lack of self-trust—the difficulty I had opening up to others. This is why when I dated Barry I'd occasionally pull back and retreat inside myself.

As a little girl I learned not to need people so badly that if they were gone, I wouldn't be able to survive the loss. I tucked that truth in my heart, and even after years of therapy and relearning better ways to process my pain, it spilled over into relationships. I could be present for others and give and give and give, but I never allowed myself to get too close. Distance, it seemed, was my trusted companion.

When I was in the hospital, all the patients had to take an art class. I couldn't see any point in this at all. I have no talent for design and wondered how this was supposed to be therapeutic. In one of our sessions, we were given a piece of clay and told to model a figure that described our lives. I sat for a while, staring at this lump of clay. I did not know where to start.

"Just do it, Sheila," the teacher said. "Don't think so much about it."

I took the clay and began to mold. When I had finished, I was surprised by what I saw. I had made a little girl who lived inside a walled circle. She looked like a normal girl except her arms were twice as long as they should have been.

"All right, class, you can stop now," the art therapist said. We were asked to walk around the room and look at one another's models, and then to say what we saw.

"Well, Sheila's is a giveaway!" someone said. "Arms long enough to reach out and help others, but no one gets to touch her." As I looked again, I saw it too: a wall that kept me safe, arms that made me useful—a lonely life.

I still struggle. Recently I spoke to an arena full of women about the storms of life. I told them we all go through them, but the aftermath looks different for everyone. Some storms knock down a tree or two. Some storms devastate the entire landscape of your life and nothing ever looks the same again.

I spoke a painful truth to the women that day. "Honestly, girls, sometimes it's easier for me to love ten thousand women in an arena than my family under one roof."

Tonight's Special

Despite my hindered ability to open up and reach out, I allowed myself to keep falling in love and continued to date Barry. We even talked about marriage. I'll never forget the night I was convinced he was going to propose. He had made reservations at the beautiful Surf and Sand Resort in Laguna Beach. I got my hair done and bought a stunning little black dress. That night I looked as good as I ever looked, ready for the big moment . . . that never came.

Two weeks later, on a Friday night, Barry asked if I wanted to go out to dinner at Sorrento Grille. "Of course," I said. "Pick me up in an hour." I pulled on some jeans and ran my fingers through my hair right before the bell rang.

"Hang on a sec, Barry," I said. "I've got to feed my cat."

When I returned a few minutes later, I started babbling on and on about my fuzzy Abigail. I reached up to give Barry a kiss on the cheek when I stopped in midsentence. His appearance shocked me. He smiled meekly as beads of sweat dripped down the sides of his flushed face. "You don't look well," I exclaimed. "Let's stay in. We can order takeout."

"No, no, no," Barry insisted. "I'm fine."

I wasn't convinced. "Barry," I pleaded. "I think you have the flu." I kept trying to talk him out of having dinner, telling him how the flu was going around and he needed to just lie down, but he wouldn't listen. In fact, he seemed anxious to leave.

On the drive to the popular Laguna restaurant, Barry was acting weird. I couldn't quite put my finger on it. He was edgy, particularly irritated when we sat in bumper-to-bumper traffic for a few minutes. He also seemed distant, not fully present. My mind did some gymnastics. I wondered if Barry's odd behavior had nothing at all to do with the flu. Maybe it was something deeper, personal. *Oh my gosh*, I feared, *he's going to call it off with me. This is it, the big breakup.*

When we finally arrived, the restaurant was packed. In fact, there was a line of people out the door. I didn't think I could handle the wait any longer. Barry grabbed my hand, and we walked right past the line and into the restaurant. *This is getting even weirder*, I thought. We were immediately seated and given menus. I blankly stared at mine for about thirty seconds, wondering why on earth my favorite chicken dish wasn't on it. Then "Tonight's Special" captured my attention: "Will you marry me? I love you more than words can say."

By the time I had picked my mouth up from the floor, a camera crew had jumped out from the kitchen, colleagues he apparently hired from his studio to catch the memorable event on film. Two things crossed my mind as my eyes bounced from the written proposal on the menu to the smile plastered on Barry's face: *Heck, I look like I just climbed up an embankment after a train wreck*, and *Of course I'll marry you!*

I Do

We got married six months later on December 3, 1994, in the historic St. Matthew's Church in Charleston, South Carolina.

I was ridiculously happy that day, not nervous in the least. I remember watching my mother get her makeup professionally applied by a makeup artist friend of mine. I was pretty sure the last time she'd worn makeup was when she got married. In fact, she had the same rouge she wore that day. As the makeup artist brushed a warm rosy color over her cheeks, my mother giggled like a schoolgirl, so much so that she was playfully scolded to stay still.

Although Barry and I exchanged vows nowhere near my home or country, it felt like everything in my life came together that day because everyone I loved was there. My mother, sister, brother-in-law, and their two boys flew in from Scotland, and my brother came from England to give me away. Even my best friend since I was sixteen years old flew over to be my maid of honor all the way from Scotland.

Bagpipers and groomsmen in kilts marched proudly down the aisle blaring stirring melodies, adding a Celtic touch to the ceremony. As I entered the beautiful church that boasted soaring stained glass windows and a steeple that seemed to reach to heaven, it began to snow. Flurries light as air danced around me as I hurried in to say, "I do."

A Welcome Blessing

I only had one concern marrying Barry, who is seven years younger than I. I knew he wanted a big family. On the verge of turning forty, realistically that wasn't something I could provide. I had told him we might be able to have one child, but at my age we had to consider the possibility that I couldn't get pregnant.

After the wedding, we hit the baby track running. I remember going to Costco and buying a box of pregnancy tests (did you even know they had those things in bulk?). Every month I faithfully tested, anxiously awaiting a positive sign. Nothing.

One morning, as I was cleaning out the bathroom cabinets, I came across the last one. I laughed to myself. My first instinct was to throw it out. *Why bother?* Besides, it was probably past its sell-by date. But something made me reconsider. I'm Scottish, and naturally frugal, so I figured since I paid for it, I might as well use it. I took the test and set it on the ledge of the bathroom sink. The phone rang in the kitchen, so I answered it and chatted for a while.

I came back to the bathroom to finish scrubbing the toilet bowl and saw the stick on the ledge. *Ugh*, I thought, *that's disgusting. I can't believe I left it out.* I hastily threw it in the trash can. As it spiraled down to the bottom, I caught a glimpse of the results indicator. For some reason, it looked different. I stared at the stick as it lay facedown. *Could it be?* My heart raced, but I didn't allow the excitement to kick in. When I finally picked it up and saw the positive sign, time stood still. There was no way I was pregnant. I reasoned I must have left the stick out too long and therefore messed up the testing process.

Still, I went to the local drugstore to buy another test, just to be sure. It was positive. I still wasn't convinced. I went back to the same store, and as the woman behind the counter rang up my second pregnancy test, she looked at me and stated the obvious: "Accept it, honey, you're pregnant."

What nerve, I thought. *She doesn't even know me!* But she did make a good point. When I allowed reality to sink in, I was over the moon. I couldn't wait to tell Barry, whom I knew would share my excitement.

Over the next several days, my elation was tempered with

fear. The questions came fast. "What do I do about the medication?" "What if I'm a bad mother?" "What if the baby is broken like me?" A whirlwind of emotions left me unsettled.

I saw my therapist, who immediately took me off the meds. He reassured me that my hormones would kick in, balance my levels, and I would likely feel a whole lot better. His words provided some relief. And he turned out to be right.

I loved being pregnant, minus the three months of nausea and vomiting. I felt great, overjoyed to be able to carry a child in my belly. When the time came for us to find out the sex of the baby, Barry and I went to the hospital for the ultrasound. We were convinced our baby was a girl, and we would call her Alexandra.

We were shocked to hear the doctor tell us we were having a boy. Barry flipped out! (I had to contain my excitement as I was lying down on a bed.) My sweet husband did a victory dance, complete with moves only known to men, right next to the ultrasound machine. We left the hospital that day and drove to a baby store in Laguna Beach where we bought three blue baby outfits. We spent the rest of the day in awe, staring at the teeny-tiny boy clothes.

During the beginning of our pregnancy, Barry and I used to sit on a hill near our neighborhood where we would take our rambunctious golden retriever, Bentley, for walks. Life seemed perfect. Comfortable. Safe. We kept our lives small, private. We had everything we needed. We were in love and expecting a baby boy. It was contentment at its peak.

Barry and I would stare into the beautiful California sky as it met the tumbling ocean and pray, "Lord, what do we do?" We had no clue what our next steps would be. Barry still worked in television, but I wondered if our true calling was opening up a local antiques store.

God, of course, had different plans. He always does.

The Unexpected

A week after I had the ultrasound, my OB-GYN called. Her voice carried some alarm. "Sheila, there's something about that last blood test that I'm not comfortable with."

My fingers trembled nervously and gripped the receiver tight. "What do you mean?"

"I'm not sure exactly what it is yet, but it doesn't look good. I'd like to do an amniocentesis."

"No. I don't want to do that." I knew the risks, the potential loss of the baby. My heart sank.

My doctor stood firm. "Sheila, you're forty. Your pregnancy is already high-risk simply because of your age. And now something looks suspicious. I highly recommend you move forward with the amnio."

I reluctantly agreed. Barry and I drove back to the hospital. We were both quiet. What was there to say? As my doctor performed the procedure, I couldn't bear to look at the monitor, so I glued my eyes on Barry. Hot tears rolled down his face as he stared at the screen, making sure the needle came nowhere near the baby. I tried to take deep breaths, but was struck by the thought that only a week prior, Barry stood in the same place, doing a happy dance. Amazing how tables can turn so quickly.

A week later the doctor confirmed her suspicions and asked us to come into the office. She recommended we terminate the pregnancy immediately. Barry and I were heartbroken at the news, but we knew aborting the child was not even a remote possibility.

"We won't do it," I told my doctor, who shook her head as I spoke. "It doesn't matter if we only have him for a day."

"I'm not sure you'll even make it through the pregnancy," she responded, adding pain to an already hopeless situation.

My heart was in knots, my spirit torn. How could God snatch away this gift that He had given us? Something we didn't even think was possible? What was the point? Was it a test? A sick joke?

The following week I was on the road, doing a television interview in a small town in the middle of nowhere. The event was in the morning, and I had nothing else to do the rest of the day. I remember passing a movie theater, the only bustling attraction in town other than a Walmart. As I walked down the single-block main street, my mind consumed with the reality of losing my most precious gift, I bought a ticket for the one movie that was featured, and that just so happened to be starting the moment I walked by.

In *Jack*, Robin Williams plays a little boy with a serious aging disorder who fights to have a life worth living. I sat in the rigid, Coke-stained seats, sobbing uncontrollably throughout the movie, hands gently caressing my belly in circles. That night I prayed. "God forgive me for thinking of myself and not this child. Whatever is wrong with him, we will love this boy and give him the best life we can for as long as we can."

I hung for dear life on an emotional roller coaster for the next few weeks, vacillating between the joys of expecting a child and the uncertainty of not knowing what our baby's struggles would be, if he even survived at all.

About a month before our little one was due, my doctor called. By this point, I had started to dread hearing the phone ring. "Sheila, are you alone?"

"Yes, Barry is at work."

"Oh." She sounded disappointed. "Well, please call me back when he gets home."

"No, no, no," I practically shouted. "Don't do this. Just tell me what's going on! Please!"

She took a deep breath. "I don't know how to tell you this, Sheila, but the day your results came back a few weeks ago, the results of another forty-year-old patient came back. Your paperwork went in her chart and hers went in yours. There's never been anything wrong with your baby. I'm so sorry you had to go through this."

My immediate thought was, *Hallelujah!* But another, more sobering one quickly followed on its heels. *There's another woman out there who is getting a very different, devastating phone call.* One mother sings with joy, another falls to the floor in tears. One woman's blessing is another mother's heartache.

For the rest of my pregnancy, I focused on our baby and dreamed of coming days when I would nestle my precious boy in my arms and inhale his sweet smell.

God's Ways Are Not Our Ways

A couple of weeks before I was scheduled to give birth, I got a phone call one morning from Steve Arterburn, a well-known Christian talk-show host. He told me about this new thing he recently started called Women of Faith, a live events organization. The team consisted of powerful women like Barbara Johnson (who passed away in 2007), Luci Swindoll, Patsy Clairmont, and Marilyn Meberg. He remarked that the three conferences they did so far were successful and had received an overwhelming response and a huge crowd. Would I be interested in joining?

I didn't have to think twice. "No," I told Steve. "Thanks for the offer, but I'm not interested." I told him I would be giving birth soon, that I could hardly make it across our kitchen, never mind an airport. I also mentioned that my idea of women's ministry didn't resonate with the truth of my life. I didn't want to wear a flowery dress and get onstage offering women four neatly packaged points on how to be a better person. I had absolutely nothing inspirational to say or offer that would help anyone. So thanks, but no thanks.

Besides, when Barry and I got married, I was convinced my ministry days were over. At that point I still didn't know any Christian who struggled with depression. So for me, it wasn't much of a story to share publicly. And back in the early nineties, scandals of high-profile Christians in ministry were at an all-time high. The mentality of the church was either you were the greatest thing or the worst thing. I was pretty sure I swung toward the latter. Sadly, at the time, there was no in-between.

Steve wasn't a man to give up so quickly. "Would you at least meet with a couple of these women?"

I entertained the idea and finally said yes. My adamant *no* was seasoned with a tiny bit of curiosity.

The next week I met with Barbara, Luci, and Marilyn at Steve's office and talked with Patsy over the phone. None of these women tried to convince me why I should join Women of Faith. They didn't mention the thousands of women who showed up at these conferences. They didn't tell me how quickly the ministry was growing.

They simply shared their stories.

Barbara told me what it was like having to identify the body of her youngest son when he was sent home from Vietnam in a body bag. He had lain dead in a rice paddy for three days and was so bloated and discolored Barbara couldn't recognize him. "No, that's not my boy," she told the coroner at first glance. Years later her other son had been killed in a devastating car wreck in Canada. She made her second trip to identify the body of her child. Having done it once before, she went again, not wanting her husband to have to endure the agonizing process and the subsequent images that never left.

Patsy told me what it was like being agoraphobic. Terrified of going outside, she had spent years isolated in her house where she smoked three packs of cigarettes a day.

I remember thinking that I just might fit in here. It was clear that these women were not the heroes of their own stories. I liked them. I liked the fact they had been broken. They weren't poised in flowery dresses giving professional talks about how to be better or stronger. Their lives were about how God had met them and was faithful in the broken places. Their stories, their lives, were their messages.

In turn, I shared with these women a little about myself and my breakdown and repeated the same concerns I had told Steve, that I didn't think I had anything inspirational to say. I thought back to my time working at CBN. One of the big topics Pat and I debated frequently was that the stories we featured on air mainly centered on the people who got their answer to prayer, their miracle, or their finances instantly turned around, or they received immediate provision. The people who hadn't were never far from my mind.

I asked Pat once, "But what about the others? Don't you think it takes more faith to keep loving and serving God when you don't get the answers to prayer?"

"Sure," he responded. "But those stories are not the inspirational ones."

For years, and even sitting in Steve's beautiful office presented with what would seem to others like an opportunity of a lifetime, Pat's statement weighed heavily on my heart. What on earth did I have to offer? Sure, I had developed ways to cope with my illness, but it didn't go away. I still had my struggles. Who wants to hear about that?

I told Barbara that much. I'll never forget her response: "Do you have anything to share that's true?"

"A little bit," I replied.

Barbara smiled and knowingly nodded her head. "Then share that."

Though I felt at home with these ladies, I needed time to think, to pray, to talk to Barry. It didn't take more than a week for my spirit to settle. Barry and I both felt in our hearts it was the right thing to do. I called Steve and told him the only way I could make this work is if my family traveled with me. He agreed.

I was still terrified about the thought of telling my story publicly. I had only done it once. I figured as soon as these four women heard exactly what I had to share, they'd see for themselves the lack of audience response. They'd hear the pin drop in the silence, and they'd finally realize I was the weak link in the chain. And they'd find a sweet way of telling me thanks, but no thanks.

But before I could prove anyone wrong, I actually had to get onstage and start talking. And before I could do that, Christian Walsh would need to make his appearance.

Welcome Home, Baby Boy

My carefully detailed and strategized birthing plan pretty much went out the window when we arrived at the hospital. Barry and I had long since fantasized about this momentous occasion. At the time, my husband had a fabulous idea of playing Christmas music in the labor room. Magical, right? Reality check—there is nothing magical when you're in excruciating pain and all you can hear in the background is, "Just hear those sleigh bells jingling, ring ting tingling too."

Barry and I welcomed precious Christian Walsh on December 13, 1996. We were happier than two newlyweds on their honeymoon. Life seemed . . . complete.

While I was overjoyed at the sight of our wrinkly seven-pound, twenty-inch mound of luscious flesh and bone, I was nervous. I remember turning to Barry the next day and saying, "I don't know how to tell you this, honey, but the nurses expect us to take Christian home!" I traveled back in time to when I was a little girl and my baby brother came home from the hospital after he was born. I was so klutzy and seemed to drop everything that landed in my hands. My mother wisely made me practice carrying a watermelon around before she allowed me to hold Stephen.

Life changed for sure, in the typical ways life changes when another human being enters your life. But it was the kind of change I thanked God for every single day. I marvel as I look at Christian now, on the cusp of turning eighteen. He's a brilliant young man with a compassionate heart. I stare into his face and am transported back almost two decades earlier, when we were recommended to abort. What would life look like today had we moved forward with the doctor's advice? How deep would I struggle with this loss? How empty would our lives be without our precious son?

As I soaked in Christian's first few weeks of life, fumbling around from lack of sleep, lost in a maze of changing diapers and feeding schedules, I remembered my commitment to Women of Faith. A new chapter in my life began to quickly unfold to the one that had just opened. "Lord," I prayed, "give me wisdom to know what I am doing and the strength to do it."

It came so soft one winter's night;
I never heard the door
or felt it dance into the room
and sail across the floor.
It crept upon my shoulder
and kissed me on the head,
and joy became a friend of mine
to call me from the dead.
For so long I have felt this need
but never knew its name
until its warmth began to melt
my snow-encrusted frame.
I see a look upon my face.
I know it came to stay.

Chapter 11

Reconnecting

*Our community with one another consists solely
in what Christ has done to both of us.*

—DIETRICH BONHOEFFER

When we left the Velveteen Rabbit, he was learning what it cost to become real and the pain of the process. He was also about to discover what a rabbit was made for. He did become the boy's favorite toy, occupying the place of most importance in the nursery. But one day the boy became sick with scarlet fever.

Some adult came through and cleaned out the nursery, tossing the rabbit out in a sack of rubbish to be burned the next morning. As he lay in the sack, the rabbit wondered what use it was to be loved if it ended like this. A real tear ran down his velvet face, and a flower sprouted where it fell. Out of the blossom stepped the nursery fairy who carried the rabbit off to a place where all the "loved, real" toys lived. She put him down on the grass and told him to run.

He found that he actually had hind legs!

He gave one leap, and the joy of using those hind legs was so great that he went springing about the turf on them.

He was a Real Rabbit at last, at home with the other rabbits.

This beautiful children's story contains many profound truths. It is painful to go through the process of becoming a transparent, authentic human being. It takes time, and we do not control its schedule; that is in the hands of God. At times it seems as if the process is shut down and we are abandoned in the darkest night of our lives. Each step takes courage and faith to keep walking, especially when it looks as if the road is leading us back to roads we have walked before. In the end, however, we begin to understand what we were created for. As we continue to walk, we find others who have been made real as well, and the journey continues with them.

Jesus did not set me free so I could wallow for the rest of my life in my new freedom and joy, but rather so the grace and space that had been gifted to me would be shared with those around me.

Stepping into Ministry

I was scheduled for my first Women of Faith event when Christian was only six weeks old. It was held in beautiful Hawaii in February of 1997. As Barry and I packed for the weekend, we stood in our little one's nursery staring at each other. We had no clue what to take on the road for a baby. Using common sense, we opted to pack up half of the nursery.

The woman who picked us up from the airport drove a convertible. I stared in horror at the roofless sports car and clutched tiny Christian even tighter in my arms. *There is no way we can ride in that thing. My baby is going to blow out of the car!* That poor woman. She could barely stuff all our belongings in the tiny trunk.

Hawaii was breathtaking. As we drove down a scenic highway, palm trees swayed in the warm tropical breeze, offering glimpses of the sapphire sea. Even as I write this, I can feel how hot it was. Like sweltering, boiling, sweat-soaking-through-your-blouse hot (and I lived in California, so I was familiar with hot). I was so nervous about Christian suffering from heatstroke I constantly sprayed him with bottle after bottle of Evian water. I'm afraid I nearly drowned him.

It wasn't until I arrived at what was Women of Faith's second big arena event (the earlier events were held in churches) that the reality of what was happening finally sunk in. From the time we left California, I was consumed with Christian. Would he sleep on the plane? Would he be hydrated enough? Would he get colicky? Did I remember his favorite blanket? I hadn't given too much thought to sharing my story.

Interestingly, no one had mentioned how big the crowd would be. I had performed in front of large audiences when I was younger, but I wasn't prepared for what I saw. When we were backstage, I asked Barry to hold Christian for a moment while I snuck a peek at the crowd through a backstage curtain.

Ten thousand women packed the stadium seats. The roar rang wildly in my ears. I scanned the sea of faces and felt a rumbling in the pit of my stomach. *What on earth did I sign up for?* I couldn't stand any longer. I was about to throw up. My feet whisked me away from the sight of the crowd as fast as they could carry me to the nearest bathroom, where I clutched the sides of the porcelain throne for dear life.

A week prior Barry had taken me to a fancy boutique and purchased a beautiful tailored suit for me for this event. Being a jeans and T-shirt kind of girl, I felt out of my element wearing it. I was even worried about Christian spitting up on the expensive fabric. Now here I was, hoping none of my lunch had landed on it.

Barbara spoke before I did. I cried the whole way through her talk. It was about walking through painful experiences. I had never heard another woman share about the journey of darkness, desperately seeking direction, answers. Barbara talked about the worst point in her life, when she got in her car and sped off to a nearby bridge. She had decided it was the perfect place to end her life. The only thing that had stopped her from gunning the gas pedal and flying over the edge was the thought she might survive. "Knowing my luck," she admitted, "I was terrified I'd end up maimed or in a wheelchair for the rest of my life."

I was blown away by her honesty. Here was a Christian woman who had just confessed onstage in front of ten thousand people that she seriously considered suicide as an option. Her vulnerability offered me more courage to tell my truth.

There is a difference between saying yes to speaking in front of thousands of people and actually doing it, microphone in hand. I was terrified. Blinded by the lights and the surprising quiet that fell over the venue after I was introduced and walked onstage, I started to share my story.

I told this beautiful group of women that I grew up in Scotland where less than 2 percent of the population even went to church, so to have parents who loved God was amazing. I talked about how close I was to my dad and about his illness and what that did to me. I told them that after his death I had spent the rest of my life haunted by this huge question no one could answer. I said, "Many people struggle with questions and they have to find a way to cope. Some pop pills. Others down bottles of wine or vodka. Some hide behind fancy clothes and perfect hair. I hid in Christian ministry. It was the perfect cover. No one was going to force me to put my Bible down and do a faith intervention."

I spoke from my heart, without notes, without a well-crafted outline. And I told as much of my story that I believed at the time was relevant. After my message, someone on the Women of Faith staff pulled me aside and told me to hang out backstage in case anyone wanted to talk to me. I smiled politely and hoped she wouldn't be disappointed if she saw me later standing alone.

I'll never forget the line of women waiting to talk to me. Familiar words gushed from their hearts. "I, too, struggle with depression." "I thought I was the only one." "I don't know how to pull myself out of this darkness anymore."

I remember flying home that weekend, overwhelmed at the response. *Why didn't I know any of this before I admitted myself to the hospital? Why did I think I was alone? Why didn't anyone in Christian ministry stand up and say, "Excuse me, this is going on and it's real!"*

I felt like this ministry pulled back the dark curtain in women's lives and allowed them to tell the truth. I was able to be honest and share, and to listen to others share similar themes. I'd found a home with Women of Faith.

Worth It All

When I had been with the ministry for about two years, I received an e-mail from a pastor at a large church near one of our events. He had heard about this conference and the fact that I had publicly addressed the issue of depression. He wrote that while a large group of women from his church would be attending, his wife was not. "She struggles with depression," he penned. "She's on medication for it, but no one else in the church knows. She thinks if people find out, the news will harm my ministry. I've tried to convince her that it won't, but she doesn't believe me. Is there any way you can meet with her?"

I wasn't sure if she wanted to talk to me, but I told this pastor I was willing and would love to connect. We arranged to meet in a small room inside the arena. He brought his wife through a separate entrance so no one would see her and waited outside the doors.

I recognized the shame that physically drew in her shoulders. Her body language blared feelings of being a weak link, a failure, the only one. She sat in a metal chair someone had brought, her head down. Mumbling a weak "hello," she anchored her sight on the cold, gray concrete floor.

"You don't have to say a word," I reassured her. "You don't have to tell me anything about your story, but if you don't mind, I would like to tell you mine."

I remember the first moment she looked up, greeting my eyes as the tears trailed down her cheek. We spent more than an hour together and culminated our time on the floor in tears at the throne of grace. When she turned to leave, I watched her run like a child into the arms of her caring husband. He picked her up and held her tight, gripping her shaking shoulders and nestling his face in her neck. The image of that reunion has never left me.

I stood alone in that tiny room and whispered, "Lord, I would go through all the hell of the battle again just for her." It would be worth it.

I love the quote from a member of Alcoholics Anonymous, and it is becoming truer for me every day: "Religion is for those who are afraid of going to hell. Spirituality is for those who have been there." I've had moment after moment in my life where I experienced the holiness of human connectedness. Had I not struggled I would have never experienced these opportunities.

Religion speaks of rules; spirituality speaks of life. Jesus said, "Blessed are the poor in spirit, for theirs is the kingdom of heaven" (Matthew 5:3). Covered in the garments of religion, we are like the rich man in that we feel invincible, cushioned from the brokenness of the world. But true spirituality makes us poor in spirit; it brings us to our knees in wretched awareness of our sinful nature. We worship at the feet of the One who has made us clean—the One who took our suffering upon Himself and in whose suffering we have fellowship. Philippians 3:10 says, "I want to know Christ—yes, to know the power of his resurrection and participation in his sufferings."

Suffering changes one's view forever, especially in how we relate and respond to others. The camera guys at CBN used to tease me about what they called my "mall ministry." Quite often, people who had seen me on television would stop me in the mall and talk for a while. Sometimes they would ask me to pray for a member of their families or for personal crises. It drove friends who were shopping with me nuts, but I loved the fact that other women felt free to share part of their lives with me.

I remember wandering through the mall one evening looking for Christmas gifts for my family. I was standing at a counter, waiting to pay, when I realized someone was looking at me. I caught her eye and smiled, and she came over to me.

"I know you must be busy, and I don't want to keep you, but I would be very grateful if you could say a prayer for me if God brings me to your mind," she said. I looked into her eyes and saw such pain. I recognized that look of barely holding yourself together. "Do you have time for a cup of coffee?" I asked her. We sat down in a quiet corner, and she began to talk. She asked if I remembered reading about a terrible road accident the previous week.

Yes, I had been horrified at the loss of a man and two little children. "That was my family," she said. We sat there for a while holding hands, tears pouring down our cheeks. There was nothing to say, nothing that would make it any better. After a while, she dried her eyes and got up to leave. We embraced, and she looked deep into my eyes and thanked me. In one sense I didn't "do" anything. I didn't come up with any clever words or magic prayers. We had just sat for a while together, two people who love God, sharing the heartbreak of life and death.

The old Sheila would have prayed for that woman and hurried on, feeling self-satisfied that she had done a good thing. But having your own heart broken changes everything. This time I really *saw* her, and we touched for a moment and left knowing our only hope is the Lord.

Taking Matters into My Hands

Life kept up a pace of fury, raising a family on the road of an amazing ministry. My depression was at bay, but the bad moments always found a way in every now and again. For the most part, I felt at peace. But there was one aspect of my illness I continued to struggle with.

I always thought that psychiatric medication was such an inexact science. If I had a respiratory infection and was given medicine, I could measure the effectiveness of the pills by the fact I was getting better. But how do you do that with mental illness? Specifically, how do I know if I'm doing psychologically better and don't need meds anymore?

When Christian was about three years old, I told my doctor I was interested in living without medication. I was sure my brain had made some progress, and I wanted to try weaning myself off. Under his medical supervision, I cut my dosage in half at first, then even further, and then I began taking a pill every other day instead of daily. After a few weeks, I was med-free.

The first four weeks were heaven. I felt amazing, alive, better than I ever had before. But sure enough, I started to spin out of control. I found myself in a dark place, that same tunnel of despair that I had fought on my hands and knees to climb out of years earlier. I couldn't continue living in that desperate state, and my psychiatrist immediately put me back on the meds.

I tried again two years later. This time I had a plan. I had an inspiring spiritual motive behind my decision. I decided I wanted to be the poster child for God's deliverance. I had been a part of Women of Faith for about six years. It was time.

"Lord," I prayed, "I really don't think I need this medicine anymore. I'm just going to trust You like I always have. I came to California with no money, trusted You, and You took care of me. I got pregnant, trusted You, and You took care of Christian and me. I think this is going to be the next place to experience victory in my life."

I had my miracle all planned out. I wasn't going to tell a soul what I was doing, not even my psychiatrist or Barry. I was going to just stop taking the meds cold turkey. A year down the line, I would publicly share what I had done. It was going to be an awe-inspiring moment. The crowd would go wild. I'd write a book, sell millions, and impact that many women and more.

After three weeks, I definitely felt palpable darkness, but I attributed that space to an attack from the enemy. I was determined to press through, to claim my victory in Jesus' name.

Barry, Christian, and I were having supper one evening. Forks clanged on plates, laughter and chitchat exchanged. Christian had an open can of soda on the table. I kept eyeing it as he told us something using grand hand gestures, shifting constantly in his seat as your typical squirmy little boy.

"Christian," I warned. "Be careful with that soda. I don't want you to knock it over." He cheerfully nodded and shifted back safely into the chair. (Today, in all his seventeen years of life, I've never needed to raise my voice to scold him. It's not that I'm such a perfect mom; my son just happens to be very sensitive. If he messes up, his immediate response is to repent and make things right.)

We continued eating, and as my son clumsily reached for something on the table, he accidently knocked over the can of soda and the syrupy liquid puddled all over the table, dribbling over onto the floor.

All I did was say my son's name. But something about the way I said it or the way I looked while saying it elicited a look of fear in my boy's eyes that I had never seen before. Silenced engulfed the dinner table. My heart raced as I excused myself and headed to the bedroom, tears exploding. Sobbing while sprawled out on the floor, I picked up the phone and called my psychiatrist. I left him a message that I needed to see him the next day.

I remember thinking, *I'm not going to let my son grow up with a crazy mom just because I don't want to be on medication.* How could I even think of sacrificing my child's happiness and security because I didn't want to have to take pills or because I wanted to show the world that Sheila Walsh was med-free?

A few minutes later I heard the shuffle of tiny feet near the bedroom door and saw a piece of paper slide through the crack on the bottom. It was a note Christian had scribbled: "Dear Mom, I think you're a wonderful mom and I hope you feel better soon."

That was a significant moment in my battle about medication. (I still keep that note with me wherever I go.) And I finally came to terms with my permanent need for it. The fact is, without the meds, I find myself slipping further and further down the rabbit hole of despair. The thought of suicide is very real. Not a day goes by without that thought crossing my mind. Just as we have a Savior who gave His life for us, we have an enemy who would love to destroy that life. It is an ongoing battle.

A few years back I learned of a new form of brain imaging that can actually show the harm that illegal drugs have done to the brain as well as the onset of early Alzheimer's and the presence of depression and bipolar disorder. A good friend of mine is a physician who worked at one of two clinics where this new procedure was available.

Knowing my history and my battle with taking medication, he offered to scan my brain and compare it to that of a normal fifty-year-old. The differences were remarkable. He pointed out a particular area in my brain, which was markedly more creative, and then one region lit up in red, which explained exactly why I need medication. It was physical evidence that my brain does not produce enough serotonin for me to live well. I wasn't emotionally weak, nor did I have spiritual problems, like not praying enough for healing. This imaging made me feel more at peace. I hope medical tests like these will be made available to others who suffer from mental illness so they can better understand the science behind the disease.

The War Within

I realize depression is my battle, but every woman has one. Recently I held a small conference in a church. In one of the sessions I asked the group of women in attendance, "What would it look like if you walked through that door this morning and suddenly all your baggage became visible? I'm not talking about what's inside your handbag, but the things you've been carrying in your spirit for years. Things like shame, guilt, instances of abuse or hurt or betrayal. I think some of you would be amazed at what you're carrying. And some of you would be horrified at how long you've been carrying it."

I challenged them to think long and hard about the baggage that was breaking their backs, weighing down their hearts. Then I gave them an option—they could either take it back home with them or make a glorious exchange. They could hand their stuff over to Jesus. They could surrender their past, their questions, their fears, their doubts, their addictions, their mistakes, their unforgiveness, and in turn, receive rest.

> "Take my yoke upon you and learn from me, for I am gentle and humble in heart, and you will find rest for your souls." (Matthew 11:29)

I invited them to pray by the altar if they wanted or stay in their seats. It was a private moment between them and the Lord. More than half of the women who were seated knelt at the front of the church, pouring out their souls, voicing heartfelt prayers through tears that dripped onto the carpet. After a woman from the church closed in prayer, some of the ladies lingered around, praying or soaking in the worship songs the band quietly played.

I noticed an older woman standing off to one side. She was a beautiful woman who wore the years well. I had a feeling she wanted to say something, so I approached her and smiled. I looked in her eyes and said, "Hi. I'm grateful that you're here." I held her hand as her frail body trembled, her eyes raw from crying.

Finally, she spoke. "Sheila, I'm eighty-three years old. When I was fourteen, I was raped. I have never told another person in my whole life because I thought it was my fault. Today I gave it to Jesus. I told Him the truth and He just held me . . ." Her voice cracked as her words trailed off. I just stood there, her soft, wrinkled hands in mine, hands that had sagged carrying a weight far too heavy.

It was bad enough dealing with depression at my age and the times I lived in; I couldn't imagine what it was like for her when she was a teenager. Had she told someone about the rape, sadly, I'm pretty sure she would have stood alone. Maybe those who heard the dark secret would have refused to believe the truth. Or perhaps some would wonder what she did to encourage the rape. Maybe she was friendly. Maybe she smiled. Maybe she wanted it.

This woman gave me the overwhelming sense of the significant number of women in the church, whether they're fourteen or eighty-four, who have secrets, who are held by these dark shadows, who believe they've been spoiled, damaged, and are not good enough.

I posted a photo of a quote on Instagram recently. It read, "One woman who understands her worth in Christ can change the world."

The response was overwhelming. I think there's something to be said here. The enemy wants to keep women shamed, unsupported, and feeling like they are the weak links in the church. But God wants to help us find the courage to believe His truth, not the accusations and lies of the enemy.

When You Die to Self, You Live for Love (God)

I think about Queen Esther, a victim who gets dragged out of her home one day at the impulse of an egotistical, maniacal king who wants to find himself a new wife because he banished his old one. So many young girls believe this is a biblical Cinderella story. A poor Jewish girl becomes queen and exchanges a drab robe and dust-covered sandals for a royal crown and glass slippers. It's a wonderful tale, right? Wrong! It's not wonderful. This was not a life that Esther chose. She was forcibly taken out of her home. And as queen, she didn't even live in the same house as the king. It wasn't a marriage in love; it was a marriage created by one man's hedonistic-driven needs.

Forced to be the wife of a fool, and living a lie because she held her true Jewish heritage a secret, Esther finds herself at a moral juncture. Her uncle, the king's servant, learns of a political plot to annihilate the Jews. Only Esther can intervene on behalf of her people and beg the king to stop the pending bloodshed.

The queen's first response? Absolutely not! Who can blame

her? Approaching the king without being summoned came at a price—her very life. But when she finally understands the weight of the task at hand, she takes three days and three nights to pray and fast, to seek the face of God, to wrestle with the decision of potentially saving the hides of millions of Jews or securing her own life through silence. She enters this time of seeking thinking, *I can't do it.* But she walks out of her prayer closet with confidence and boldness. "If I die, so be it," she says.

If we, too, are willing to walk through our dark nights, we can come out on the other side different women, with a deeper relationship with God and a deeper understanding of our need for Him. Yes, we will lose ourselves in the process. We will die to what holds us back, what keeps us under, what makes us afraid. And we will gain something greater.

As Paul said, "I have been crucified with Christ and I no longer live, but Christ lives in me. The life I now live in the body, I live by faith in the Son of God, who loved me and gave himself for me" (Galatians 2:20). By the time Esther stands before the king, she is dead to what makes sense to her.

And you can't scare a dead woman.

God uses this one woman to destroy a deadly political scheme and save the fate of millions of Jews. The king ruled a vast empire. If Esther had kept quiet and not risked her life, every Jew on the planet would have been annihilated. Did God want a teenage girl ripped out of her home to marry an egotistical maniac? Absolutely not! But could God use her in that position? Absolutely!

Does God want any woman to have both her breasts removed because of cancer? No. But can He use her in that place? Absolutely!

Does God want a woman to suffer at the hands of a physically abusive husband? No. But can He use her because of that situation? Absolutely!

Does God want a woman to end up in a psychiatric hospital on the verge of suicide? No. But once she's there, can God use her? Absolutely!

God in Everything

God can use the very things that the enemy intends to use to destroy us to connect with others and Himself in ways we would have not otherwise been able to. That's what happened with Joseph when he stood before his brothers who had sold him into slavery when he was a teenager. That one decision to destroy Joseph's life turned into a roller coaster of blessings, like working in the royal palace and being promoted as the Pharaoh's right-hand man, and plights, like being mistreated, falsely accused of rape, and even thrown into prison for years.

I find it interesting that at every turning point in Joseph's life we read this phrase, "And God was with Him." I especially love what he says to the very men who had left him for dead in an empty cistern so many years earlier. Not wanting to exact revenge or seep in bitterness, Joseph told them, "You intended to harm me, but God intended it for good" (Genesis 50:20).

Joseph was an innocent man who had been seriously wronged, and his story has relevance for us all. If we have committed our lives into God's hands, we can trust Him that even the worst storms will be used to make us more like Christ.

Revelation 12:11 says, "They triumphed over him by the blood of the Lamb and by the word of their testimony; *they did not love their lives so much as to shrink from death*" (emphasis added).

There is such freedom in dying to what makes sense to us and trusting God with our future—no endless questioning, just waiting on His next instruction. He will give us courage, and with each step that courage will love us back to life.

Love falls gently on each wound
Like snow upon the frozen ground
And life that seemed a distant dream
Will waken in the promised Spring

Chapter 12

Broken, but Held Close, Never Forgotten

The LORD is close to the brokenhearted
and saves those who are crushed in spirit.

—PSALM 34:18

I started out on this journey with the best intentions in the world—to love and serve God—but somehow, somewhere, I took a wrong turn and got lost. I found my way but in the process was left broken.

I grew up in Scotland with sheep all around me, field after field of white wool and incessant crying echoing throughout pastures. Of all the lessons I have learned from these defenseless, gentle animals, the most profound is the most painful.

Every now and then, a ewe will give birth to a lamb and immediately reject it.

Sometimes the lamb is rejected because it is one of twins and the mother doesn't have enough milk or she is old and, frankly, quite tired of the whole business. If the lamb is returned to the ewe, the mother may even kick the poor animal away.

They call those lambs "bummer lambs." Unless the shepherd intervenes, that lamb will die. So the shepherd will take that little lost one into his home and hand-feed it from a bottle and keep it warm by the fire. He will wrap it up with soft blankets and hold it to his chest so the bummer will hear a heartbeat. When the lamb is strong, the shepherd will place it back in the field with the rest of the flock. "Off you go now, you can do this, I'm right here."

The most beautiful sight to see is when the shepherd approaches his flock in the morning and calls out to them, "Sheep, sheep, sheep!"

The first to run to him are the bummer lambs because they know his voice. It's not that they are more loved; it's just that they believe it. I am so grateful that Christ calls Himself the Good Shepherd.

> He calls his own sheep by name and leads them out. After he
> has gathered his own flock, he walks ahead of them, and they
> follow him because they know his voice. (John 10:3–4 NLT)

I am a bummer lamb. Chances are you are too.

I've come to accept the fact that I'll be broken as long as I'm on this earth. I used to think that at some point God would fix me and my testimony would be a great story for other people. I don't think that will be true anymore. And I'm at peace.

I think most of us will carry with us the reminders of being broken. We bear scars from a painful divorce, the loss of a loved one, the grip of addiction, the negative report from the doctor. Oh, God will help and strengthen us in the process. We will learn a lot more. And we'll have a greater understanding and empathy for each other because of it. But until we see Jesus face-to-face, we'll be broken.

But this is no longer the bad news; it's the best news! We don't need to waste our time continually pointing out what's wrong with us or what's wrong with our lives or what happened to us that's plain wrong; we can spend our time on earth concentrating on what's gloriously perfect about Christ and sharing that revolutionary news with the world.

We can dare to believe Him. We can dare to immerse ourselves in His love. We can dare to stay so close to Him that we never forget the sound of His gentle voice.

The Essence of Life

God gives each one of us unlimited resources in Christ to rise above small earthbound dreams and live lives that reflect eternity in our hearts. But it is hard, even heartbreaking sometimes, to step out from behind our masks and be known, to step out of the shadows and share our truth. But even though it is hard now, it will be much harder if we leave it until later. In *Mere Christianity*, C. S. Lewis said that "the cowardly thing is also the most dangerous thing." He used the example of a mountain climber facing a climbing task that is very hard to do, but is also the safest thing to do. If he bypasses it, hours later he will be in far worse danger. Lewis went on to say,

> It may be hard for an egg to turn into a bird: it would be a jolly sight harder for it to learn to fly while remaining an egg. We are like eggs at present. And you cannot go on indefinitely being just an ordinary, decent egg. We must be hatched or go bad.[1]

When there is something physically wrong with our bodies, we accept that to be healthy we have to deal with the problem. People who ignore the body's warning signs don't always get a chance to live to regret it.

It is the same with our hearts and our souls. God in His compassion gives us signs that all is not well, but it is much easier to ignore them and just keep walking. A sickness in our souls is much more dangerous than a weak heart or a few cancer cells. I do not want for a moment to minimize the pain and trauma of disease, but when our hearts are at peace in Christ, we can say with Paul, "For to me, to live is Christ and to die is gain" (Philippians 1:21). What is most tragic is to never really live at all. Perhaps your own path is strewn with the garbage of the past. Many adults today are held hostage by childhood traumas with which they cannot make peace.

I ask you with all my heart to open yourself to embarking on the only journey that leads to life. As long as you have breath in your body it is never too late. If, like me, you have buried your anger and shame for so long that you are severely depressed, there are many wonderful Christian treatment centers and godly counselors available. Or ask a trusted friend to recommend someone. There is nothing to be ashamed about in reaching out for help. It takes a lot more courage to step out into the darkness than to stay in the prison in which you may currently be living.

Many people are afraid to get help because they fear it may cost them too much. And it may—it may cost you everything you once thought you valued. That very fear ran through my mind time and again before I decided to get help. What if in reaching out for help for myself I discovered I was no longer welcome to reach out to others? My whole life had been focused on being a minister of Christ's love to a broken world. I now believe that is one of Satan's lies to keep us from finding deep love and acceptance in Christ. I've discovered that our brokenness is a far greater bridge to others than pretend wholeness ever is.

One of the letters I received after appearing on *The 700 Club* to say good-bye was from a well-known Christian speaker who wrote to me from a drug and alcohol rehab center. He said he had lived in misery for years, torn between the success of his work and the devastation in his private life. He had wanted to get help many times, but knew it might cost him everything. He had finally found the strength to walk away from the addictive spotlight to a place where he could be made whole. His letter reminded me of the words of the martyr Jim Elliot: "He is no fool who gives what he cannot keep to gain what he cannot lose."

If your husband or wife or someone you love is in trouble, dare to reach out to him or her as well. Sometimes we are afraid to do that in case we cannot put the pieces back together again, but it is much worse to deny a problem until the whole thing explodes and the pieces are scattered to the far corners of the earth.

Mental illness affects families, not just the person dealing with it. When I married Barry, he didn't understand the depths of my pain. Even to this day, he is learning more and more about the disease as remnants make their way in at times. He has learned to make peace that it is God who will take care of me, not him; that God is the only one who can give me peace.

There are fears and questions you may have as you watch your loved one struggle. It's not an easy thing to witness or understand. And while you may not be able to fix the problem, make things right, or end the battle, your presence and support is crucial.

The Essence of Life

I know that someday I will stand before almighty God and give an account of my life. I have made many mistakes that Christ has graciously covered with His blood, but the greatest mistake of all would have been to ignore the call to come out of the darkness and show myself. We can continue to take care of the outside of our lives, or we can turn away from what will not last and ask the Lord to show us who we really are.

I spent a lot of time grieving over the picture of who I am without Christ. I will not forget it, and I have asked God in His mercy to never let me banish that picture from my mind. It may seem like a nightmare to face all that is true about ourselves, but when we combine it with the glory of who we are in Christ, it is a gift that will take us through the night until the morning breaks.

I was invited to speak and sing some time ago at a retreat for staff and key supporters of the ministry of my good friend Joni Eareckson Tada. In the worship service on the final morning, a man slowly made his way to the podium to read the Scripture. Born with cerebral palsy, he had been through years of speech therapy and was now willing to read in public. He read from 2 Corinthians 12:7–9: "I was given a thorn in my flesh, a messenger of Satan, to torment me. Three times I pleaded with the Lord to take it away from me. But he said to me, 'My grace is sufficient for you, for my power is made perfect in weakness.'"

As I listened to this man read, I saw with my own eyes the truth of those verses lived out in front of me. Flying home that day I realized that we are all "disabled"; it is just more noticeable with some of us than others. Some of us are blind or in wheelchairs, while others of us are angry and bitter. What matters is what we are going to do with our disabilities. If the man who had battled cerebral palsy had kept himself locked away, embarrassed by his disability, he would never have brought so much to us during the service that day. Only in surrendering ourselves to living transparent, accountable lives can we be God's picture show to one another and to the world—a visible, tangible demonstration that God is real.

I know it is hard to change after having lived one way for so long, but it is not too late; you just have to seize the moment and begin. You are not alone. Christ will be with you every step of the way. There is a place for each person that no one else can fill, and there is something you bring with you, when you step out of the shadows, that no one else can bring. Perhaps, like me before I began my own journey, you feel you are locked inside a prison. But just beyond those prison doors there are people who are cheering you on. If you'll just try the door, I think you'll find that it is open.

> *Prayers are heard when children pray,*
> *though sometimes it takes years*
> *to find the strength to listen*
> *to the truth behind the tears.*
> *Her body grew, as children do;*
> *inside she lived alone,*
> *a little girl,*
> *her spirit bruised and trapped beneath a stone.*
> *But one day in her prison cell,*
> *a tiny shaft of light*
> *began to burst through bars of steel*
> *and lift the dead of night.*
> *And as the little girl looked up*
> *she saw herself all grown*
> *and the hand she took*
> *that led her out*
> *looked strangely like her own.*

The man at the pool of Siloam waited for thirty-seven years for someone *else* to help him. Then Jesus came along and said to him, "Pick up your mat and walk" (John 5:8). Often we have wasted much of our lives waiting for someone else to take that first step of healing for us. I say to you, in Jesus' name, "Rise up and walk! Come out of the shadows, and step into the light. You were not created to merely survive, you were made to live. And only Christ can truly love you back to *life!*"

Notes

Chapter 5: Why Are You Afraid?

1. Quote from C. S. Lewis, *The Lion, The Witch and the Wardrobe*, (New York: HarperFestival, 2005), 79–80.
2. Eleanor Roosevelt, *You Learn by Living* (New York: Harper, 1960), 29–30.
3. Thomas à Kempis, *The Following of Christ*, Book 3, chapter 17.
4. Eugene Peterson, *Answering God* (San Francisco: HarperSanFrancisco, 1989), 98.

Chapter 6: Paralyzed by Shame

Epigraph: Lewis B. Smedes, *Shame and Grace* (New York: HarperCollins, 1993), 3.

1. Quoted in Smedes, *Shame and Grace*.
2. George MacDonald, "The Last Farthing," *Unspoken Sermons Series II*, public domain.

3. Quoted in Mrs. Charles E. Cowman, *Streams in the Desert* (Grand Rapids: Zondervan, 1996), 70.

Chapter 7: *The Longest Night*

1. John of the Cross, cited in *Devotional Classics*, ed. Richard Foster (San Francisco: HarperSanFrancisco, 1990), 34–35.

2. Thomas à Kempis, quoted in *The Treasury of Catholic Wisdom*, ed. John A. Hardon (San Francisco: Ignatius Press, 1995), 359–60. Also see *Imitation of Christ Book II*, "Admonitions Leading to the Inner Life: 9"; "Of Lack of Solace and Comfort," (II.9), 87.

3. C. S. Lewis, *A Grief Observed*, 1961, chapter 1, page 1.

4. C. S. Lewis, *The Problem of Pain* (New York: HarperCollins, 1940/1996), 91.

5. John Bradshaw, *Healing the Shame That Binds You* (Deerfield Beach, FL: Heath Communication, Inc., 1988), 118.

Chapter 8: *Forgiveness Comes Full Circle*

1. Charles Spurgeon, *Treasury of David: A Commentary on the Psalms*, 3 Vol. (Peabody, MA: Hendrickson, 1988), 3:119.

Chapter 9: *Following the Shepherd*

1. Michael Quoist, *With Open Heart* (New York: Crossroad Publishing Company, 1983).

2. Bob Benson and Michael W. Benson, *Disciplines for the Inner Life* (Nashville: Thomas Nelson, 1995).

Chapter 12: *Broken, but Held Close, Never Forgotten*

1. C. S. Lewis, *Mere Christianity* (New York: HarperCollins, 2009), 198–99.

About the Author

S heila Walsh is a powerful communicator, Bible teacher, and best-selling author with more than 5 million books sold. A featured speaker with Women of Faith®, Sheila has reached more than 5 million women by combining honesty, vulnerability, and humor with God's Word.

She is the author of *The Storm Inside*, the best-selling memoir *Honestly*, and the Gold Medallion nominee for *The Heartache No One Sees*. The *Gigi, God's Little Princess* book and video series has won the National Retailer's Choice Award twice and is the most popular Christian brand for young girls in the United States. Sheila cohosted *The 700 Club* and her own show, *Heart to Heart with Sheila Walsh*.

Twitter: @SheilaWalsh
Facebook: facebook.com/sheilawalshconnects
Instagram: Sheilawalsh1

Available Now

The Storm Inside

Trade *the* Chaos *of* How You Feel *for the* Truth *of* Who You Are

SHEILA WALSH

Available Now

STUDY GUIDE
GROUPS / INDIVIDUALS

EIGHT SESSIONS

The Storm Inside

Trade *the* Chaos *of* How You Feel *for the*
Truth *of* Who You Are

SHEILA WALSH